The Living Earth Manual of Feng-Shui

Stephen Skinner graduated from Sydney University, majoring in philosophy, geography and English. With this balance of arts and science he has brought to his research into feng-shui both the logical techniques of a geographer and the understanding of the mystical side of feng-shui.

Having worked as a lecturer in geography he migrated to the United Kingdom in 1972 to further his research into the work of John Dee and the earlier magical manuscripts in the British Museum. It was here that he became interested in geomancy and feng-shui. Several trips to the East put him more firmly in touch with modern practitioners of feng-shui, especially in Hong Kong, Bangkok and Singapore where experts in this field are consulted by even the largest building companies on projects ranging from new towns to office blocks. He has carried out extensive field work and has worked on a number of feng-shui consultations in collaboration with Chinese feng-shui practitioners. He now works as a magazine publisher and lives in London.

Stephen Skinner's books include *A Narghile of Poems*, *The Search for Abraxas* (with Nevill Drury), *Techniques of High Magic* (with Francis King), *Terrestrial Astrology: Divination by Geomancy* and *The Oracle of Geomancy*. He has edited *Aleister Crowley's Astrology*, *Aleister Crowley's Tao Teh King*, *In Pursuit of Gold*, *The Magical Diaries of Aleister Crowley* and *The Complete Enochian Dictionary*.

STEPHEN SKINNER

THE LIVING EARTH MANUAL
of *Feng-Shui*

Chinese Geomancy

ARKANA

ARKANA

Published by the Penguin Group
27 Wrights Lane, London w8 5tz, England
Viking Penguin Inc., 40 West 23rd Street, New York, New York 10010, USA
Penguin Books Australia Ltd, Ringwood, Victoria, Australia
Penguin Books Canada Ltd, 2801 John Street, Markham, Ontario, Canada l3r 1b4
Penguin Books (NZ) Ltd, 182–190 Wairau Road, Auckland 10, New Zealand

Penguin Books Ltd, Registered Offices: Harmondsworth, Middlesex, England

First published by Routledge & Kegan Paul plc 1982
Published by Arkana 1989
1 3 5 7 9 10 8 6 4 2

Library of Congress Cataloging in Publication Data

Skinner, Stephen 1948–
The living earth manual of feng-shui.
Bibliography: p. 137
Includes index.
1. Feng-shui. I. Title.
BF1779.F4S58   133.3′3   82–3845

ISBN 014.01.91127   AACR2

Made and printed in Great Britain by
Richard Clay Ltd, Bungay, Suffolk
Filmset in 11/13 pt. Monophoto Plantin

Contents

Illustrations

TABLES

LINE DRAWINGS

Acknowledgements

My thanks to Bob Lawlor who first indicated the existence of feng-shui to me, and to Helene, who put up with me while I researched the subject.

I also wish to acknowledge the aid of the librarians at the British Library, the Warburg Institute, the Wellcome Library and S O A S. My thanks also to John and Françoise Nicholas who acted as my correspondents in Hong Kong, where some of the last practitioners of this ancient art still carry on a flourishing trade. Together with Beth McKillop, they helped me with materials only to be found in Chinese.

My especial thanks to Nick Tereshchenko who gave me my first feng-shui compass, to Beverly Lawton and Lindsay Roberts who typed the first manuscript, and to Evelyn Lip for her help whilst I was in Singapore, although the fruits of this research came too late for inclusion in this book.

The drawing of the dragon and tiger schema is reproduced by permission from the *Annals of the Association of American Geographers*, vol. 64, no. 4, 1974, p. 508, fig. 2, Chuen-yan David Lai. The drawing of the simple lo p'an comes from Henry Doré's *Researches into Chinese Superstition*, T'usewei Press, Shanghai, 1914, whilst the full lo p'an is used as an illustration by J. J. M. De Groot in *The Religious System of China*, Brill, Leiden, 1897.

Early Chinese sources include the map of a hsüeh from the *Luan t'ou chih mi*, vol. 4. Using the feng-shui compass in the Ching dynasty appears first in *Shao Kao*. The elemental forms of the mountains are attributed to Kuo P'o in his classic *C'iu t'ien hsuan nu ch'ing-nang hai-chiao ching*, the nine moving stars appear in the *Ti-li ta-cheng*, vol. 1, and the river formation is drawn from the *Shui-lung ching*.

The Chinese house plans are reprinted from *Under the Ancestors' Shadow* by Francis L. K. Hsu with the permission of the publishers, Stanford University Press, copyright of 1948 and 1967 by Francis L. K. Hsu.

The author and publisher wish to thank the Hong Kong Government Information Service and the *South China Morning Post* for their helpful co-operation.

Etymological note on geomancy

'Geomancy' is really a misnomer for the Chinese practice of *feng-shui*, as the word more properly relates to an Arab form of divination which spread north into Europe and south into Africa at the end of the first millennium. The word 'geomancy' was, however, adopted by writers of the mid-nineteenth century (*c.* 1870) to translate *feng-shui*. The present work treats of feng-shui, or telluric geomancy, and is concerned with the location of dragon lines of energy in the earth and their interaction with man as part of his subtle environment.

'Feng-shui' has been used in preference to 'geomancy' to describe this ancient Chinese art throughout this book. Its unrelated cousin, divinatory geomancy, has been the subject of two previous books by the author.

Although feng-shui (wind and water) is the most often found and most colloquial Chinese name for the theory and practice of siting attuned to the elements, the name which is most consistently used in classical Chinese sources is *ti li* ('land patterns' or in modern times 'geography'). This emphasizes the fact that the Chinese saw feng-shui not so much as a superstitious branch by itself of rural practices but an integral part of the study of the land itself and the patterns on it both natural and man-made.

A third and perhaps older term is *kan-yü*, which literally means 'cover and support', or even 'cover and chariot', referring to the heaven and the earth. It encompasses the old resonance theories of traditional Taoist philosophy which held that actions on earth affect the heavens and movements in the heavens act upon the surface of the earth.

Although in the great Chinese encyclopedias feng-shui is listed under the kan-yü chapter, it is likely that originally the two practices were quite distinct. Kan-yü was possibly the original designation of the Compass School, whilst feng-shui was probably the early designation of the Form School. It is only in later years that the distinction has become somewhat muddied, although a distinction still survives in Taiwan. Just taken literally, kan-yü means 'chariot of Heaven and Earth' and refers to the round Plate of the compass (Heaven) set into the square Earth Plate of its holder (a feature which many compasses now lack), while feng-shui refers, obviously, to the natural elements which would be more the concern of the Form School.

Wheatley in his *Pivot of the Four Quarters* considered feng-shui to be an 'astro-biological mode of thought', reflecting the Chinese idea that life (in all its forms) interacts with heaven and is modified and conditioned by the cycle of the five elements.

Steven J. Bennett in his article 'Patterns of the sky and the earth: the Chinese science of applied cosmology' in *Chinese Science* (1978, 3:1-26) prefers to call feng-shui 'astro-ecology', which sounds rather modern and perhaps doesn't cover all of the aspects of feng-shui. Bennett also likes to refer to it as siting theory, which gives it a rather geographical flavour.

Introduction

The ancient Chinese art of feng-shui or geomancy lies behind the whole pattern of the Chinese landscape. It is an attitude to the life in the land that has enabled China to feed one of the densest populations in the world without doing great violence to the earth.

Although China is a predominantly agricultural country, the Chinese art of living within the rhythms of the land and the seasons is just as applicable to life in the Western world. Although the system of feng-shui is intrinsically linked to traditional Chinese Taoist philosophy, the practical tenets are universal.

Just as yoga cultivates the life-force in man in both the East and the West, so feng-shui can cultivate the life-force or *ch'i* in the earth as easily in the West.

Ch'i flows through the earth like an underground stream which varies its course according to changes made by nature or man to the surface of the earth, although the underground streams which can be observed during caving expeditions are not the same as ch'i. A parallel can be drawn with the flow of ch'i through the acupuncture meridians of the body. These meridians are not the same as the blood vessels which can be dissected by the surgeon's knife, but convey life energy through their own specific locatable channels.

Nevertheless the effectiveness of acupuncture has been admirably demonstrated to the satisfaction of Western medical practitioners on numerous occasions. According to the practitioners of acupuncture, their practice relies upon locating these, as yet undissected, meridians and modifying the flow of ch'i through them.

To complete the parallel, the practitioners of feng-shui manipulate the surface of the body of the earth to influence the flow of ch'i along its hidden veins or dragon lines. The feng-shui expert is therefore commonly referred to as a *lung kia* or 'dragon man', as he traces or 'rides' these veins of ch'i from their source high in the mountains (the mythical abode of dragons) to the lower slopes where they affect for good or ill the people living on or near them.

Consequently the art of feng-shui consists in trapping and pooling beneficial ch'i or deflecting malefic ch'i from the site chosen. The pooling of good ch'i brings not just agricultural fertility but a fertility of the environment, a locale suitable for living free of the background of unease often associated with living quarters in cities, suburbs or individual dwellings built contrary to the prevailing flow of life in the land, or whose 'atmosphere' has been muddied by conflict both human and natural.

Such conditions can often be restored to peace by the manipulation of the environment by a 'dragon man'; as, by analogy, a body can be restored to health by the regularization of the acupuncture meridians.

The parallel between the body and the earth has not been chosen as an arbitrary metaphor but reflects the Chinese view of the wholeness of the universe not divided rigidly into the categories of Western theology (matter and spirit) or science (living and dead). Instead the 'dragon man' looks upon existence as a continuum, much as C. G. Jung saw the universe: the external macrocosmic world being reflected in the internal microcosmic world.

After all, who can deny that the adjustment of the environment, by methods no more esoteric than the addition of landscaped parklands to a city or the decoration and refurnishing of a room, reflect upon the lives of the inhabitants?

The rules of feng-shui apply equally to the siting of a

whole city, or even a province, down to the arrangement of the living space in the smallest bed-sit in the heart of that city.

I

Wind and water: what is
feng-shui?

To be in the right place facing the right direction doing
the right thing at the right time is, then, a cross between
being practically efficient and being ritually correct. It is
being in tune with the universe.

Stephan Feuchtwang

Many look for their Shangri-la on the surface of the earth,
others voyage within for illumination. The ancient Chinese
art of feng-shui combines the axes of each quest, declaring
that what you make of your location and environment on
the face of the earth also affects your interior peace. The
formula relies upon locating and harnessing the 'dragon
lines' of energy which pass through the veins of the earth,
affecting the quality of life upon its surface in varying
degrees.

Popular Chinese religion, based on the pre-Confucian or
Taoist times, centred around ancestor worship and a veneration of various spirits of the place not unlike early Greek
beliefs. In China these beliefs became overlaid by other
more abstract philosophies whilst the original beliefs still
retained their strength amongst the peasants and those
closest to the soil. In Greece the early animistic beliefs
helped generate the later complex mythologies which were
the basis and the classical roots of European culture. Chinese animistic beliefs spawned the various observances and
practices such as feng-shui which are unique to China.

The landscape teemed with life: demons, guardians, spirits of mountains, pools, springs, trees and rocks, in fact of

any prominent feature of a locality. All of these could become objects for veneration, fear or placation. Life was not confined merely to that defined as living by biology, but pulsed through the rocks, waters, earth and winds. The whole universe was seen as a living organism.

Chinese art depicts this feel for the spirits of the land, and portrays one or two salient features, which live and breathe to the exclusion of all else, often in splendid isolation in space or cloud. Western art fills in all the background, with a passion for leaving no space. Similarly, Western architecture is hell-bent on fitting in as much as possible into a nice neat rectangular grid which is carved into the ground by bulldozers: it takes no care with the siting of each unit, cuts out any clusters of unique, eccentric or erratic buildings, and emphasizes only the practical, never the beautiful: such is its formula. The Chinese, however, could no more build houses or villages which cut unthinkingly into the flesh of the landscape than would a surgeon operate without looking at the patient's body.

It is easy however for Western 'developers' to slash their way across the countryside in the name of the great god 'Motorway', or create new towns without any more thought to the underlying land than is required by the plumber.

To add to the landscape one must create not a thorn in its flesh but a form which flows and breathes with the rhythm of the earth in which it is planted. Wood and stone taken from nature are to be hewed and fitted back into nature. Pagodas, houses, temples, towns or hamlets in China are all part of the earth and were built as such. It is only since the Revolution and the consequent industrialization of China that some synthetic materials, discordant forms and shapes have grown up. Only since then has function or productivity sometimes taken priority over peace and harmony with the living land.

The art of living in harmony with the land, and deriving the greatest benefit, peace and prosperity from being in the right place at the right time is called feng-shui.

Feng (wind) and Shui (water) make up feng-shui (pronounced somewhat like 'foong-shway'). Together they express the power of the flowing elements of the natural environment, and this power is expressed in, and derived from the flow of energy not only on the surface, which has been sculpted by wind and water, but also through the earth. Placing oneself in a favourable feng-shui environment will bring good fortune, peace and a longer life.

Often people who do not know why it is so, feel 'at home' in one environment but not in another. Apart from the obvious environmental factors such as type of house or neighbours there is also the more subtle effect of the interaction of that person with the feng-shui environment. Where in new developments there is a feeling of bareness and sterility, it is because the wound caused in nature has not had time to heal over. Where the violence done to nature is great, or the elements introduced so out of accord with the landscape, the wound will never heal. Many large Western cities, particularly their more modern sections, have done so much violence to the underlying earth that it is doubtful if it will ever 'accept' the new structures, perhaps not till they lie in ruins and nature has again claimed them. Ruins often induce a kind of melancholic euphoria, at least if one visits them alone. This euphoria is also a function of the environment related to the final acceptance by nature of man's previous intrusions.

During the nineteenth and twentieth centuries, Europeans in China came up against the phenomena of feng-shui. The Chinese regard for the life of the land manifesting in feng-shui, forced missionaries to remove the tops of their churches and railway builders to change the course of their railways, in accordance with this Chinese interpretation of the balance of the hidden forces in the landscape.

The inherent Chinese belief in feng-shui was so unquestioned that many of the early clashes left the Chinese bewildered that the 'foreign devils' who wished to build spires, railways and other incongruously straight structures should be ignorant of the basic principles of nature.

Historically China has always looked upon itself as the

well-balanced 'Middle Kingdom', the centre of the habitable world. A consistent foreign policy of several millennia which cut China off from the rest of the world has reinforced this view, only now being consciously broken down at the political level.

A naïve result of this is that traditional Chinese geography insisted upon all rivers flowing eastwards (as indeed most do in China), and also that all the highest mountains, the source of the rivers, were located in the west. Additionally, this formalized geography pictured the south as the quarter of the greatest warmth and hence of the greatest good, whilst most of the cold winds (feng) blow from the dark north.

Accordingly all Chinese maps were orientated with the quarter of greatest goodness, the south, at the top of the page. We will follow this convention (the opposite of Western cartographic procedure), identifying north at the bottom of the page, east on the left and west on the right. Although this takes some getting used to, there are some symbolic benefits to thinking in the Chinese mode: and it certainly makes the comprehension of feng-shui texts significantly easier.

So, from the position of the viewer in the north, the world, city or site under consideration is orientated as shown in Figure 1. Southwards is also the direction in which many of the waves of invasion have flowed over China. The four animals traditionally attributed to the compass quarters are coloured in a way which reflects their geographic/climatic attributes.

Given this orientation, and apart from the rules of feng-shui, it is common sense to protect one's habitation from the bitter winter winds of the north, and encourage the balmy airs of summer and the south. If prosperity was ever linked with health, then the theory behind feng-shui certainly has a factual enough foundation in China!

Following the convention of 'as above, so below', Chinese geographers identified the basic regions of their country with the various constellations of the night sky said to rule

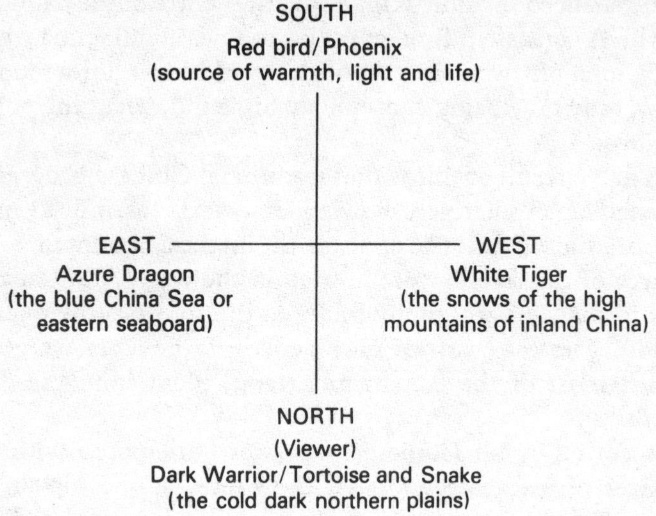

SOUTH
Red bird/Phoenix
(source of warmth, light and life)

EAST ——————————————— WEST
Azure Dragon   White Tiger
(the blue China Sea or   (the snows of the high
eastern seaboard)   mountains of inland China)

NORTH
(Viewer)
Dark Warrior/Tortoise and Snake
(the cold dark northern plains)

Figure 1 Orientation of the site and relationship between the
animal symbols of the cardinal points of the compass

them. Obviously this creates some overlap between astronomy, geography (ti li) and feng-shui, inevitable in a system
which sees mutual interaction as an essential feature of a
living universe. Within this theoretical framework are to be
found a number of practical, sociological, siting and even
sanitary considerations (such as are not far removed from
the minds of modern city planners).

The macrocosmic view of the interrelation of the constellations and the geography of the whole Chinese empire is
reflected in the more pragmatic approach to the effects of
certain stars upon towns or individual dwellings.

Dwellings are divided into those of the living (houses)
and those of the dead (graves and tombs), for the Chinese
see no break between the living and the dead in terms of
family or ancestral relationships.

At the same time there is a microcosmic/macrocosmic
axis to consider, so that the field of action of feng-shui can
be laid out as shown in Table 1. Although much of the

Table 1 Macrocosmic and microcosmic siting of the living and the dead

	Yang Chai (Houses) location of the living	Yin Chai (Tombs) location of ancestors
Macrocosmic	Country or empire City or town House	Tombs of the Emperors Clan temples Tomb
Microcosmic	Orientation of the rooms of the house	Orientation of the tomb

available feng-shui lore concerns the Yin Chai or grave locations, most of these rules can be extrapolated to explain the intricacies of Yang Chai siting. Likewise the rules for city orientation are also of use in the siting of individual houses.

The Two Schools of Feng-Shui

Superimposed on this classification are the two main schools of thought in feng-shui, the Form School and the Compass School. The former and the older of the two is concerned with the visible form of the landscape surrounding the site under consideration, be it a Yang Chai (house) or a Yin Chai (tomb). The Compass School, however, is concerned with a time axis and a complex set of relationships between 'sensitive' directions as indicated by an elaborate many-ringed compass.

Each of the two schools has a number of designations, the most common of which are:

1 Form and Configuration School (*hsing shih*), also known as the Shapes School, Kanchow method and Kiangsi method (the latter being an indication of its geographical

origins, and the dwelling-place of its patriarch, Yang Yün-Sung). It flourished in Kiangsi and Anhui provinces and is today referred to as the 'mountain peaks and vital embodiment school' (*luan t'i*) or intuitive approach.

2 Directions and Positions School (*fang wei*) or Compass School, also referred to as the Fukien School (its probable province of origin and home of Wang Chih, one of its early major proponents), the 'Method of Man', or 'Houses and Dwellings Method'. In Chinese it is often designated the *tsung miao chih fa* (Ancestral Hall) method, the *li ch'i chia* (according to Shen Hao), or the Min School. It flourished in Fukien and Chekiang provinces, and in Taiwan and Hong Kong where it is referred to as the ch'i pattern school (*li ch'i*) or analytical approach.

By the late nineteenth and early twentieth centuries, the two schools were no longer separate and distinct. Feng-shui men practised both methods of siting in both Fukien and Kiangsi, according to De Groot, but they maintained that there was still a clear demarcation between the two styles. Obviously the mountainous areas of the south (Kwangsi) are more susceptible to the Form School, whilst those who lived on the flat plains needed the compass to detect favourable directions in an otherwise unremarkable and featureless landscape.

The Form School: Yang Yün-Sung

Yang Yün-Sung (or Shuh-Meu as he is sometimes called, *c.* AD 840–*c.* 888) was an Imperial feng-shui master or *hsien-sheng* to the Emperor Hi-Tsung from 874–888 and a native of Kwangsi province, who spent most of his life in Kiangsi. Both from his widespread fame and the works he wrote, he has always been regarded as the patriarch of the School of Forms. He laid particular stress on the shape of mountains and the direction of water courses, and the influences of the dragon which play a considerable part in his system under various names and aspects. The titles of three of his writings are consequently concerned with dragons: *Han Lung Ching* or 'Classic on the Art of Rousing the Dragon', usually referred to as the 'Classic of the Moving Dragon'; *Ch'ing-Nang Ao-Chih* or 'Secret Meanings of the Universe'; *I Lung Ching* or 'Canon for the Approximation of Dragons' – this refers especially to those forms and outlines of nature where dragon and tiger do not prominently stand forth and are, as it were, concealed. *Shih-Erh Chang-Fa* or 'Method of the Twelve Stave Lines' which has become a classic for the determination of the *hsüeh* or 'lair' of the Dragon in which it is most favourable to build or bury, is included in the *Ch'ing-Nang Ao-Chih*.

The Form School was the first to be formally established and is the most naturally based, taking into account the configuration of the surrounding landscape as seen from the site of the building or the grave.

Compass School: Wang Chih

Not until the rise of the Sung dynasty (AD 960) were all the elements of feng-shui gathered into one system, built firmly on a philosophical basis and developed methodically, so as to combine every form of influence which heaven may be said to exercise on earth and which both heaven and earth were supposed to have on human affairs. Under the influence of the metaphysical speculations of the Sung dynasty a second school of feng-shui arose which more particularly laid stress upon the *kua*, the eight trigrams, the Heavenly Stems and Earthly Branches and the Constellations (more of which later), assigning a place of minor importance to the actual configurations of the earth. The chief representative of the Compass School, Wang Chih (also named Chao-khing or Khung-chang) spent the latter period of his life in the north of Fukien province where he wrote his 'Canon of the Core or Centre' and his 'Disquisition on the Queries and Answers', both of which were published by his pupil Yeh Shuh-liang.

The Ming dynasty writer Wang Wei (1323–74) sum-marizes the position of the two schools and their background in the *Lung heng* as follows:

The theories of the geomancers [sic] have their sources in the ancient Yin-Yang school. Although the ancients in establishing their cities and erecting their buildings always selected sites [by feng-shui], the art of selecting burial sites originated with the *Tsang shu* ('Burial Book') in 20 parts, written by Kuo P'o of the Chin dynasty . . . In later times those who practised the art divided into two schools.

One is called 'tsung miao chih fa' [Compass School]. It began in Fukien, and its origins go far back; with Wang Chih of the Sung dynasty it gained currency. Its theory emphasizes the Planets and the Trigrams; a yang hill should face in a yang direction, a yin hill in a yin direc-tion, so they are not at odds. Exclusive reliance is put on the eight Trigrams and the five Planets, which are used to determine the principles of generation and destruction. The art is still preserved in Chekiang, but very few people employ it.

The other is called the Kiangsi method (Form School). It started with Yang Yün-sung and Tseng Wen-ti of Kanchou, and its doctrine was refined especially by Lai Ta-yu and Hsieh Tzu-i. Its theory emphasizes landforms and terrain (hsing shih) taking them from where they arise to where they terminate, and thereby determining position and orientation. [Practitioners] give their whole attention to the mutual appropriateness of dragons, sites, eminences, and waters, obstinately refusing to discuss anything else. Nowadays [during the Ming dynasty] south of the Yangtze, everyone follows it.

The Form School utilizes a greater degree of intuitive insight whilst the Compass School, although more complex in its theory, is more subjective and mechanical in applica-tion. As Chao Fang (in *Tsang shu wen ta*) expressed it:

'In the Form School the principles are clear but the practice is difficult . . . with the Compass the principles are obscure but the practice is easy.'

The rationale of the manual for 'Yang dwellings' is by now apparent, but the reasons why graves should be sited with care according to feng-shui principles is less obvious. Basically it is necessary to appreciate that for the Chinese the ancestor was a very important person and kinship and family group ties were much closer than those experienced in the West. Extended families or clans living together, often with three or more generations under the same roof, reinforced this attitude, so that the relocation of a grand-parent was more important (when their status changed to that of dead ancestor) than was their location whilst they were living.

Further than this, the more distinguished ancestors or clan leaders became objects of veneration, both to make sure that they continued to look with favour upon the living, and also because their status as spirits gave them considerable power over the fortunes, fate and circum-stances of the living. This power of course was more specifi-cally directed to blood-line relatives, consequentially atten-tion to the comforts of the ancestor was a most important part of Chinese ritual.

Oddly it was even thought that ancestors could be 'mani-pulated' by good feng-shui to benefit their descendants by the accumulation of ch'i whether the ancestors wished it or not.

A belief intrinsic in the system of ancestor worship, which pre-dates Taoism or Confucianism in China, is that the souls of ancestors are linked with the site of their tombs. As they also have a direct effect on the lives of their descendants, it follows logically that if their tombs are located favourably on the site of a strong concentration of earth energy or ch'i, not only will they be happy but they will also derive the power to aid their descendants, from the accumulated ch'i of the site. As Eitel (1873:21) puts it:

the fortunes of the living depend in some measure upon the favourable situation of the tombs of their ancestors. If a tomb is so placed, that the animal spirit of the deceased, supposed to dwell there, is comfortable and free of disturbing elements, so that the soul has unrestricted egress and ingress, the ancestors' spirits will feel well disposed towards their descendants, will be enabled to constantly surround them, and willing to shower upon them all the blessings within reach of the spirit world. So deeply ingrafted is this idea of the influence of the dead upon the living, that Chinese wishing to get into the good graces of foreigners will actually go out to the Hong Kong cemeteries in the Happy Valley, and worship there at the tombs of foreigners, supposing that the spirits of the dead there, pleased with their offerings and worship, would influence the spirits of the living, and thus produce a mutual good understanding between all the parties concerned.

Consequently the art and science of feng-shui is of prime importance for locating the best-aspected site for a grave as this decision affects the fortunes of all the deceased's children and their families.

As Chinese belief included at least three spiritual principles or souls as well as the physical body, it was necessary that each be laid to rest with the utmost care; one soul (p'o) remains in the grave with the body, benefiting from the hopefully good feng-shui of the site, one in the ancestral tablet of the household altar (by which link the benefits of the feng-shui of the burial site affects the family), and one soul (hun) in the other world, purgatory or paradise, more or less beyond the reach of the feng-shui influences.

From John Blofeld's excellent Taoist work *Beyond the Gods* comes a story which illustrates the intimate connection between the soul in the grave, in this case suffering from an ill-thought-out burial, and the soul in the ancestral tablets who is free to roam the house and affect his descendants.

The other story ... had been told me in all seriousness by a Malayan Chinese student during our undergraduate days at Cambridge. While still too young to comprehend the fact of death, he was told by his parents that his grandfather had passed away. It was hard for him to understand why his daddy and mummy looked so upset; for death, whatever that might mean, had not changed Grandfather in any special way; he was often to be seen wandering about the house at night, looking grumpy just as usual. But when his daddy came to hear of this, he grew dreadfully pale and said something like: 'Alas, dear boy, your Gran must be in terrible distress, otherwise his restless spirit would have left this house forever. Next time you see him, be sure to ask.'

Unafraid, the innocent child questioned his grandfather at their very next encounter.

'My boy, you can have no idea,' replied the ghost. 'I can find no rest at all. The gate-keepers of the Chinese heavens chase me away, declaring there is no admission for people dressed in European-style clothes like this white drill suit in which your father so thoughtlessly clothed my corpse. At the Christian heaven, it is the same. The guards drive me off because someone once forgot to sprinkle holy water on my forehead. Now nothing is left for me but to wander unendingly among those unhappy shades who, being childless, have no descendants to offer sacrifices before their tombs, which is really quite unfair considering I begat no less than seven sons. They do offer sacrifice, but I never get a whiff because the essence of the food and drink is wafted straight to heaven.'

When the child reported this problem to his parents, the old man's body was hurriedly exhumed and the unsatisfactory white drill suit exchanged for a Chinese robe, whereafter the ghost was never seen again!

Ancestor worship takes place on the 1st and 15th day of every lunar month as well as the anniversary of the death of the ancestor concerned. 'Worship' is actually a misleading term as there is no thought that the ancestor has become a god (although some of the imperial ancestors did) but that filial duty or genuine affection is being expressed, and beyond that, the limited power of the ancestor to help or hinder his living descendants has to be propitiated or even pandered to.

The filial duty which partly motivates ancestor worship is an extension of the Confucian ethics which became the basis for imperial law under which respect for elders, dead or alive, was a cardinal duty. Thus, not only was ancestor 'worship' designed to promote the favour of the ancestor, but also to build up a supply of grace from regular application of this Confucian precept. This 'worship' took the form of supplying the soul of the ancestor with the necessaries which he required in life: food cooked and cut up is laid out with chopsticks and much kowtowing in front of the ancestral tablet. The tablet acts almost like a talisman for storing the soul of the ancestor. The ritual is carried out by the head of the family and for the benefit of the family.

One typically Chinese dread, exemplified in Blofeld's anecdote, is that their line of descendants will dry up and there will be no one to look after the needs of their soul. In this case the soul becomes a 'hungry ghost' who becomes generally vindictive and preys on travellers. He may eventually need to be exorcized, like a demon, by a monk or priest.

The fear of neither being able to receive the ancestral offerings nor having any descendants to offer them is very real. Hence the importance of a good feng-shui burial which leaves the p'o in a comfortable habitation, and ensures that there are plenty of fortunate descendants to continue the worship and sustain the hun of the ancestor.

No less important is the selection of a site for the home of the living or the re-arrangement of its rooms to improve its occupant's eventual happiness, health and wealth.

2
Earth's blood: ch'i

The fraction of the Earth's magnetic field produced by outside sources is now understood to be an important representation of the electromagnetic activities in the Earth's upper atmosphere ... the daily varying part of the Earth's magnetic field can be ascribed to electric currents flowing in the Earth's upper atmosphere.

Article on the magnetic field of the Earth
in *Encyclopaedia Britannica*, vol. 6, 1974

Whichever school of thought is followed, the main objective is the clarification of the ch'i content of a site. Ch'i has no equivalent in Western terminology, except perhaps for the Hebrew *ruach* which has been translated 'breath of life'. Ch'i is the active energy which flows through the forms produced by *li*. As such it is responsible for the changes in form which is a characteristic of all living beings, and that includes the earth itself.

Ch'i acts at every level – on the human level it is the energy flowing through the acupuncture meridians of the body; at the agricultural level it is the force which, if not stagnant, brings fertile crops; and at the climatic level it is the energy carried on the winds and by the waters.

The various forms of ch'i include *sheng* ch'i or vital ch'i, and *ssu* ch'i or torpid ch'i. The former is Yang ch'i and the latter Yin ch'i, so that sheng ch'i flows most readily during the hours of the rising sun (midnight to noon), whilst ssu ch'i prevails during the declining hours of the sun (from noon to midnight). As the sun moves from east to west, the compass points from which one can expect either sheng ch'i or ssu ch'i alternate. Just like the tides ch'i ebbs and flows, not only throughout the day but also throughout the seasons of the year and within the framework of the sixty-year cycle upon which the Chinese calendar is based. Consequently determining the current state of ch'i flow related both to the clock and the calendar is important when beginning an enterprise which could be affected by the state of ch'i, for example, building, altering, moving, buying or selling property. This is simply expressed by the 'Site Classic' which explains how important it is to act when there is a flow of vital ch'i which will energize the biosphere of the site:

> Every year has twelve months, and each month has positions in time and space of vital and torpid ch'i. Whenever one builds on a vital ch'i position of a month, wealth will come his way and accumulate . . . To violate a monthly position of torpid ch'i will bring bad luck and calamity.

The interrelation between time, space and ch'i is explained in the 'Site Classic' in terms of the twelve terrestrial Branches (*ti chih*) and the ten celestial Stems (*t'ien kan*) used to mark the passage of time. The terrestrial Branches mark the twelve double hours of the day and the twelve directions of the compass. Combined with the ten celestial Stems they form the cycle of 120 *fen-chin*, which also caters for the 60-day and 60-year cycle of the Chinese calendar. (These terms are explained in Chapter 4.)

Hence there is a change in direction and quality of ch'i flows every two hours of the day and these ch'i flows are not exactly repeated for the next 60 years. Consequently exact determination of the best starting time for any venture which might involve ch'i – and this extends to activities other than building – is quite an exacting science.

For the Compass School of feng-shui the interaction of the Stems and Branches with time and space are very important. However, the Form School thought of ch'i more in terms of its 'pneumatic circulation' and looked upon the circulation of ch'i almost in the same way that the modern geographer looks upon the hydrologic cycle. Just as the water evaporates off the surface of oceans and rivers and ascends to the sky before condensing and falling again as rain to make those very rivers, so the circulation of ch'i fluctuates between heaven and earth. When vital ch'i is congealed or accumulated it encourages growth of all kinds beneficial to mankind; where it is dispersed there is barrenness and where it has gone torpid there is death and decay. Each is a natural phase in the circulation of ch'i, and it is for us to take advantage of this cycle just as the farmer takes advantage of the climatic changes through the year and plants crops in spring and reaps in autumn rather than attempting the reverse which would of course be disastrous.

Just as a farmer might look for a spring of fresh water so you can locate or encourage the welling up of ch'i from the ground. Such points occur best where there is a change of landform, a bend in the river or the change from plain to scarp, or the meeting of a Yang and a Yin landform. In each case this natural node is modified by the surrounding flows of wind and water.

To understand feng-shui it is essential to appreciate ch'i. On a microcosmic level, ch'i is the energy of the body's breath which if concentrated in various parts of the body can enable the practitioner to perform the more amazing feats of the Chinese martial arts schools.

What is true of the microcosm is also true of the macrocosm, and ch'i is naturally accumulated and may be enhanced at certain points in the earth by the application of landscape alterations made in accordance with feng-shui rules.

In *Tao Magic*, Laszlo Legeza (1975, p. 13) explains ch'i:

Ch'i, the Vital Spirit, fills the world of the Taoist. It is the Cosmic Spirit which vitalizes and infuses all things, giving energy to man, life to nature, movement to water, growth to plants. It is exhaled by the mountains, where the spirits live, as clouds and mist and, therefore, the undulating movement of clouds, mist, or air filled with smoke rising from burning incense, is a characteristic mystic representation of ch'i in Taoist art.

Note the emphasis on clouds and mist, the feng and shui, forming dragons in the air. It emphasizes the connection between ch'i and feng-shui. To continue:

As the Universal Force or Eternal Energy, it is at the centre of Taoist breathing exercises, which also involve the art of smelling and the use of incense. In occult diagrams it is the reason for the preference for asymmetrical design. The 'Pao-p'u tzu' states: 'Man exists in ch'i, and ch'i is within man himself. From Heaven and Earth to all kinds of creation, there is nothing which would not require ch'i to stay alive. The man who knows how to circulate his ch'i maintains his own person and also banishes evils that might harm him.'

This refers to the inner cultivation of the Taoist sexual alchemy.

The same source mentions a method of casting spells by simply rendering breath (ch'i) more abundant. The Taoist Chao Ping used to charm streams by breath so that the water-level dropped as much as twenty feet. Using the same technique, he would light a cooking-fire on thatched roofs without setting light to the dwelling, render boiling water harmless for scalding and prevent dogs from barking.

This is the magical application of ch'i which is at the base of all Taoist magic, details of which can also be found in John Blofeld's *The Secret and the Sublime*.

As ch'i pervades both Heaven and Earth, the ch'i are divided into:

1. Earth ch'i (*ti ch'i*) or host ch'i who have their life in the dragon veins of the earth. These run through the earth and along its watercourses and are subject to decay. They are governed by the Later Heaven Sequence of the trigrams.

2 Heaven ch'i (*t'ien ch'i*) or guest ch'i are affected by the state of t'ien and may overrule the effect of Earth ch'i. These are governed by the Former Heaven Sequence of trigrams.

3 Weather ch'i of which there are five, mediate between Earth and Heaven ch'i much in the same way that man is midway between Heaven and Earth and has some small say in influencing both. The five weather ch'i are rain, fine weather (or sunshine), heat, cold and wind. Significantly these weather ch'i, including wind or feng and rain or shui are the movable ch'i, the fluctuating elements distributed between the more fixed ch'i of Heaven and Earth. Thus the ability of feng-shui to judge or control the ch'i of Heaven and Earth is admirably reflected in the presence of feng and shui amongst the intermediary weather ch'i. Not only do the weather ch'i mediate between Heaven and Earth ch'i, but they partake of the nature of both. They are subject to decay like the Earth ch'i and are governed by both sequences of trigrams. Their decay is governed by the fluctuations of ch'i which is usually described as 'the advancing and the reverting breath'.

The cyclical flux of ch'i is described by a series of characters called the Twelve Palaces which describes the rise and wane of ch'i energy in a human life-cycle, but is equally well applicable to the waxing and waning of the ch'i of a site (see Table 2).

Just like the tides of the sea, it is as necessary to receive the influx of life on the incoming tide as it is to lose the waste and detritus on the outgoing tide. This is why the dragon and tiger must be balanced, with the incoming tide of the dragon in the ascendant so that the positive virtues of ch'i gradually accumulate rather than being washed away (which would be the case if the Yin tiger predominated).

Table 2 The Twelve Palaces

1	shou ch'i	受氣	to receive breath
2	t'ai	胎	womb
3	yang	養	nourishment
4	sheng	生	growth, or to be born
5	mu yu	沐浴	to be cleansed
6	kuan tai	冠帶	to come of age (literally to assume cap and girdle)
7	lin kuan	臨官	to approach officialdom (become an official)
8	wang	旺	prosperity
9	shuai	衰	to decay (become weak)
10	ping	病	to become sick, sickness
11	ssu	死	to die, death
12	tsang	葬	to be buried, burial

The two breaths of nature are, however, essentially one breath. The male and female principles, uniting, constitute the beginning of things; when they disperse they cause decay, dissolution and death.

When the breath of ch'i is exhausted in the human body, it dies. When it is abundant feats of almost superhuman strength and skill can be performed. It is obviously very important for one's living space to be supplied with an adequate accumulation of ch'i. The adept of internal alchemy or the martial arts has learned to accumulate ch'i in his own body by a hard and exhausting regimen, but for most of us the degree of passive absorption of ch'i from our surroundings, be they home or work, is the factor governing our energy and lucidity level. An increase of ch'i in a site automatically benefits those living there, and feng-shui provides a method of doing this.

The image is clear: the greatest generation of ch'i occurs at the point where the loins of the dragon and the tiger are locked together in intercourse. The sexual nature of the spot where there is some 'sudden transition from male to female' is the link between ch'i as applied to the body of the earth and ch'i as applied to the body of man: in each case it is the same force which is generated by sexual intercourse.

Ch'i interpreted as generative energy explains why the siting of graves is important for the continued fecundity of the descendants of the occupant of the grave, whose families should multiply vigorously if the feng-shui of the grave is well judged.

Now as there is only one point of sexual contact between the two ranges of hills coupling in the form of tiger and dragon, it is obvious that the supply of prime feng-shui sites is extremely limited, especially as owners of such sites were careful to prevent the occurrence of any other burial or building nearby which might draw off the valuable ch'i. Other sites on the two ranges of hills are purely tributary ch'i sites, just as the various meridians of the body carry a flow of ch'i but none so strong as the *haru* or the genitals themselves.

The Taoist practitioners of sexual yoga and internal alchemy called their art the yoga of the azure dragon and white tiger. The parallel is quite explicit, and not merely symbolical.

How do we interpret the mating of these two symbolic animals? To understand this, it is necessary to consider the nature of the dragon. The Chinese dragon may be understood in many senses: the animal of the eastern quarter, the transmogrified immortal, or in the feng-shui sense, the writhings of the landscape and the form of mountain ridges. The ridges and lines in the landscape form the body, veins (*lung mei*) and pulse of the dragon whilst the watercourses and pools and underground watercourses form the dragon's blood. The veins and the watercourses both carry the ch'i, the life-force of the Earth. Of course, lines of trees, roads and even railways carry or disperse ch'i across the landscape. The geometry of the flow of ch'i can be amazingly complex, forming a lattice or a network between the main dragon veins, for no part of the earth is dead. Some parts are barren and some are stagnant, but none are totally dead.

The amount of ch'i flowing, and whether it accumulates or is rapidly dispersed at any particular point, is the crux of feng-shui. An auspicious site or hsüeh (dragon's lair) needs to be near a good strong flow of ch'i, but not necessarily on the main vein or artery, which may even carry away its beneficent influences almost as fast as it brings them! A splitting into many and branching streams of ch'i is also a disadvantage, just as sheet drainage of water can do as much damage to the surface of the earth as a raging channel torrent. Oddly the parallels between an agriculturally desirable drainage system and the most effective flow of ch'i are remarkably consistent. The two critical elements of the landscape from a feng-shui and an agricultural point of view are the mountains (*shan*) and watercourses (*shui*): all else is formed by their interaction. As Feuchtwang neatly puts it, 'shan and shui are merely positive and negative of the same thing; the shan follow the same lines as shui since every shan is the back of a shui – taking shui in its broadest sense . . . whether dry or with water running in it.'

Just as the Chinese approach to geography meshes with the more mystical feng-shui, so their approach to meteorology invokes the aid of the weather ch'i in explaining the seasons. The weather ch'i produce, under the combined influence of the five planets and the five elements, the twenty-four seasons, which are called the 'twenty-four breaths of nature'. The ch'i allied to the element wood, and guided by Jupiter, produces rain (*shui*); combined with the element metal and ruled by Venus, the ch'i produces fine weather; joining the element fire and influenced by Mars, the ch'i produces heat; supported by the element water and ruled by Mercury, the ch'i produces cold; and with the help of the element earth and influenced by Saturn, it causes wind (*feng*).

So goes the theory of Chinese meteorology, which sees the

state of the season as an index of the current relationship between Heaven and the Earth or Man. Any climatic prodigies therefore will indicate a breakdown in the smooth functioning of this relationship, rather like Shakespeare's use of climatic disturbances in *Macbeth* to indicate the world's outrage at the murder of a king.

How then does this impinge on feng-shui? The trained feng-shui hsien-sheng will note carefully the response of the weather ch'i to his client's arrival on the selected site to see if the two are compatible. Further, the feng-shui hsien-sheng will try and determine *a priori* the best season for his client to take up residence, so that the then ruling weather ch'i will be in full accord with both the main features of the site and of the horoscope of its prospective occupier.

When this delay is applied to the burial of the dead, it has not been uncommon for the bones of an immediate relative to remain unburied for some considerable time awaiting the auspicious season. In fact in Amoy during the last century missionaries used to refer to the jars of bones which dotted the hillsides awaiting a more propitious disposal as 'potted Chinamen'. This practice, although actively discouraged, has persisted in some communities to this day, especially among those families who feel they must also save up for an appropriate burial.

But to return to the question in hand: how may we determine the exact location of the flows of ch'i and whether any particular dragon vein is favourable or unfavourable, fast-flowing or slow-eddying, and whether tapping a particular spot will result in an accumulation of the precious ch'i?

First it is useful to know that where there is a true dragon, there will be also a tiger, and the two will be traceable in the outlines of mountains or hills running in a curved course. Moreover, there will often be discernible the dragon's trunk and limbs; even the very veins and arteries of his body running off from the dragon's heart will appear in the form of ridges or chains of hills.

As a rule, there will be one main accumulation of ch'i

near the dragon's genitals, whilst near the extremities of his body the ch'i is likely to be exhausted. At a distance of twenty li (six miles) the breath becomes feeble and ineffective. But even near the dragon's heart, the ch'i unless well kept together by surrounding hills and mountains, will be scattered. Where the frontage of any given spot, though enjoying an abundance of ch'i, is broad and open on all sides, admitting the wind from all the four quarters, there the ch'i will be of no advantage, for the wind will scatter it before it can do any good.

The essence of good feng-shui is to trap the ch'i energy flowing through the site and accumulate it without allowing it to go stagnant.

One of the classics of feng-shui says that ch'i rides the winds and disperses, so that windy sites unprotected will lose any accumulated ch'i. However, when bounded by water the ch'i halts. Here are the two elements of feng-shui, wind and water. The wind if tamed to a gentle breeze will bring the circulating ch'i, the water if curved and appropriately oriented will keep the ch'i in the site thereby increasing its physical and spiritual fertility. The third main consideration is not to allow the ch'i to go torpid or stagnant in which case it becomes ssu ch'i.

If these three things can be achieved by the natural configurations of the landform, then the makings of an excellent lair (hsüeh) have been discovered. If this lair has the appropriate balance of Yin and Yang landforms then the necessary energy exists to attract the ch'i.

The site is referred to as a lair because the selection of a dwelling site or house is as essential to man's well-being as the selection of a lair is to an animal. While the animal instinctively selects his dwelling-place, man has lost these instincts and needs some guidance such as that provided by feng-shui.

An ideal site, therefore, is one protected from high winds by a northern screen of hills or trees, a place in which streams and rivers meander slowly, and which nestles in the embrace of hills rather like an armchair, with a view preferably to the south. The horseshoe shape which is repeated many thousands of times in Chinese cemeteries is an artificial representation of the ideal protecting ranges to the rear of the site. The Ming tombs north-west of Peking reflect such an ideal configuration in a natural landform which was obviously selected for that purpose. The lair is usually the nucleus of a more complex system of dragons (lung) which extends outwards from the lair.

Although there are a number of favourable sites in any dragon configuration, only one will be the perfect site which is where it is considered that the white tiger of the west and the blue dragon of the east interlock sexually. In any given landscape a number of possible points can be located for this, but according to tradition only one of these, which will be infinitely superior to the other, will be the true point of sexual union. To live in such a site (or perhaps to bury one's ancestors there) guarantees a life rich in spiritual and physical benefits: a site paralleled by the image of the pearl being chased by the dragon.

However, feng-shui, pragmatic as ever, acknowledges that most of us lay our heads in less exalted lairs and consequently provides numerous rules for improving upon their ch'i collecting properties.

The forms and configurations should be looked upon as the body of the dragon; the water and underground springs, the blood and veins of the dragon; the surface of the earth, the skin of the dragon; the foliage upon it, the hair; and dwellings as the clothes, according to the 'Huang-ti Chaiching' or 'Site Classic'. Along the lines of the ridges, both blown by the wind and carried by the water, as well as through the underground channels, flows the vital ch'i which feeds the life on the surface of the earth. The direction from which this ch'i flows colours it with different qualities – some of them conflicting, some of them complementary. To determine the resultant mix of these ch'i flows the site is often looked upon as a disc or compass card with flows of ch'i entering or leaving from various directions. One school of thought particularly lays stress upon the exact degrees of entry and exit in relation to the centre. Obviously if you move some distance from the site under consideration, your new location will stand in a different relationship to the flows of ch'i which now enter at a different angle. This Compass approach differs from, but is complementary to, the Form School approach which relies more on the intuitive assessment made by the practitioner of the forms of the dragon.

Sha

Although the site should not be windy or exposed as this will result in the dispersal of ch'i, conversely if the site is completely hemmed in so that the air does not circulate or the water nearby is sluggish and stagnant, the ground literally gives off damp and stinking exhalations (sha), rendering the place unfit either for living inhabitants (for very obvious as well as feng-shui reasons), or for the burying of the dead (as the corpse would not last long under damp conditions).

The preservation of the coffin and the bones in the grave was considered very important. It was even asserted that grave sites with a large accumulation of ch'i, with the bones of the ancestor well preserved, not only reflect benefit on his descendants but also sometimes actually radiate a luminous glow up through the earth, which is supposed on occasion to be visible. Hence very practical considerations of the right type of soil and drainage system have become part of the lore of feng-shui.

Detailed specifications of the type of soil are given by De Groot (1897: 953):

hollow, flat or straight-lined formations do not respire, and are therefore of little or no use for burying or building purposes. In making graves, attention should also be paid to the fact that hard, rocky soil is breathless; compact, reddish loam on the contrary is full of breath and life and consequently prevents a quick decay of the coffin and the corpse, rendering the bones hard, white, and suitable for binding the soul for a long time to the grave. Besides, white ants and other voracious insects are not harboured in such loamy soil, which fact geomancers ascribe to the influence of ch'i.

It is interesting to note the element of compulsion in the binding of the soul to the grave, as a necessary prerequisite for good feng-shui for the descendants of the soul so bound.

If watercourses near the place run off straight and rapidly, there the ch'i is also scattered and wasted before it can serve any beneficial purpose. Only in places where the ch'i is 'well kept together, being shut in to the right and left, and having a drainage carrying off the water in a winding tortuous course', are the best indications for accumulating ch'i.

Taking together all these factors so far outlined we have formed a picture of the conditions necessary for locating the best spot for the accumulation of ch'i known to the feng-shui hsien-sheng as the 'dragon's lair'. This useful term designates either the tentative site under consideration, or more accurately, a site whose properties have been determined and which satisfactorily accumulates the ch'i.

Sha is the antithesis of ch'i and can be translated as 'noxious vapour'. It is a form of evil ch'i and is often called sha ch'i or feng sha (noxious wind).

Sha can be produced by a configuration of the landform which leads to the loss of good ch'i or actively promotes evil ch'i, or it can be generated by conflicting influences and conjunctions as determined by the compass. It can also literally refer to a cold wind issuing from the earth (marked by hollows) or through gaps in the protecting mountain ranges to disturb the accumulation of ch'i and render the site inauspicious.

'Secret arrows' are straight lines which by virtue of their power to conduct ch'i pierce any accumulations of ch'i and reduce its efficacy. These lines can be straight ridges, house tops, railway embankments, telegraph wires or any set of parallel straight lines aligned with the spot which is subject to the evil influence of these 'secret arrows'. These are a specific form of sha. Such 'secret arrows' can be blocked off from a site by a wall, row of trees, embankment or octagonal 'target boards' with the appropriate deflecting characters written thereon.

As a general rule, which is reflected in the intricacies of Chinese art, the meandering undulating line conducts ch'i whilst the straight line, sharp bend or fast watercourse indicates sha. In some ways the organic lines are as typical of Chinese civilization as rectangular Descartian lines are the hallmark of Western civilization. Basic to the nature of feng-shui dragon lines and Chinese civilization generally is the curve as opposed to the straight line which expresses itself not only in Western architecture, but also in the ley lines which it has often been suggested are the European equivalent of dragon lines. They are in fact diametrically opposed. Straight lines, as we have seen, are anathema in feng-shui for they generate sha and 'secret arrows' and let in demons.

The configuration of many Chinese towns and villages owes its evolution more to the avoidance of sha than to the European obsession with 'the shortest distance between two points'. The larger cities such as Canton and Peking, although featuring square-gridded streets, are adequately protected as a whole by their correctly aligned city walls and compensatory statues and pagodas.

As a general rule, as straight lines of ridges or chains of hills produce malign influences, so do straight creeks, canals or rivers. As water is looked upon as the emblem of wealth and affluence, where water runs off in a straight course it causes the property of those dwelling there to run off and dissipate like water. Tortuous, crooked lines are the indication of the possibility of a beneficial ch'i accumulation.

It is interesting that there are definite geographical advantages to a site found to be in accordance with the rules of feng-shui. For example, quite often straight (arrow-like), fast-flowing rivers are located along fault lines. Sharp bends which are also inauspicious often indicate underlying structural defects and irregularities. Heavily meandering rivers, however, are likely to be found where there are large deposits of fertile alluvial sediment: good land to settle. Similar parallels in fact give a substantial common-sense background to the dragon-lore of feng-shui.

Although some sites may look auspicious by all the rules of feng-shui so far outlined, the possibility of noxious exhalations, sha, or 'hidden arrows' should always be looked into. Essentially, sha is the poisonous opposite of ch'i. Continuous straight lines are generally considered to be an evil indication. A typical example might be a line formed by rooftops of the same height pointing in the same direction. Any Western city will provide innumerable examples of this sort of line. Likewise a scarp face rising up in a bold straight line is conducive to the production of sha.

Fortunately, in general the existence of sha or a pernicious breath will betray itself by outward indications. It is said that whenever there is a hill or mountain, rising abruptly up from the ground, running in a straight line, or showing an exceedingly rugged appearance unmitigated by any gradual sloping or Yin influence, then one can expect to find dangerous breath there. Generally speaking, all straight lines are evil indications, but most especially when a straight line points directly towards the spot where a hsüeh has been chosen.

Even suppose a place has been found where both the dragon and the tiger are united, each curved like a bow, but with the side ridges running in straight lines (resembling an arrow laid on the bow), then that would be an absolutely dangerous configuration, all the more so for the apparent perfection of the site.

The symbolic arrow will puncture and wound the dragon vein, thereby leaving it to fester and produce sha, a fanciful interpretation perhaps, but one taken very seriously by all feng-shui hsien-sheng, particularly the exponents of the Form School for whom the visible manifestations of the landscape are paramount.

Not only the direct arrow line was to be feared, but also the straight street or railway line which if directed across the frontage of a site will effectively drain it very rapidly of its accumulated ch'i.

It is in fact this aversion to sha which caused in colonial days in China the purchase and subsequent destruction by a Chinese syndicate of one particular piece of railway track which ran straight toward a city whose livelihood it was assumed to be damaging. Straight railway embankments and similar works were looked upon with much disfavour in China.

Straight waterways, a formation that is very uncommon in nature anyway, are also avoided, especially as water is such a good conductor of ch'i. Water is symbolic of wealth and a straight stretch of it leading from a site will, according to feng-shui, promote the rapid loss of wealth.

Another curious feng-shui contra-indication is the presence of free-standing rocks or boulders. If they are integrated with the landscape by being well screened by trees, shrubs and moss then their discordant note is muted, but should they be exposed and uncovered, they will destroy the flow of beneficent ch'i and make for an ill-aspected site.

There are many tales of tombs located in such a neighbourhood whose influence continued to be beneficent till accident, climate or the deliberate act of a malicious enemy uncovered the boulders or felled the trees, resulting immediately in a sudden misfortune, loss of wealth or disgrace falling upon the descendants and their families. Such accounts have done a great deal to reinforce belief in feng-shui.

Hong Kong, where many of the mainland Chinese feng-shui hsien-sheng retired after the Revolution, is endowed with an abundance of free-standing rocks and boulders scattered about the hillside of the main island, causing it to abound with sha. The associated phenomena of loosely held soil slopes has resulted in a systematic tree-planting effort by the government, which is accordingly credited with considerable forethought in the matter of feng-shui, as trees

are supposed to help mitigate this particular noxious
breath.

The early design of Government House with its curved
and sweeping drive, good aspect and backing by a cordon
of trees, has done little to disabuse the populace of their
suspicion that the colony's engineer and architects were in
fact master feng-shui hsien-sheng. Anecdotes about the
early feng-shui clashes between government and missionaries on the one hand and the populace on the other,
abound, but perhaps one of the most interesting (it being a
sort of negative feng-shui) is related by Eitel (1873:53):

The most malicious influence under which Hong Kong
suffers is caused by that curious rock on the edge of the
hill near Wanchai ... The Chinese take the rock to
represent a female figure which they call the bad woman,
and they firmly and seriously believe that all the im-
morality of Hong Kong, all the recklessness and vice of
Taip'ingshan are caused by that wicked rock. So firm is
this belief impressed upon the lower classes of Hong
Kong that those who profit from immoral practices
actually go and worship that rock, spreading out offerings
and burning frankincense at its foot. None dares to injure
it, and I have been told by many otherwise sensible people
that several stonecutters who attempted to quarry at the
base of that rock died a sudden death immediately after
the attempt.

Just as the authorities could modify the influence of the
rock near Wanchai by systematically planting a tree screen
round it, so, for a price, an inventive feng-shui hsien-sheng
can allay or modify the worst effects of sha or 'secret
arrows'.

The standard method in the latter case is to build a feng-
shui wall or screen to cut off the sight of the offending
quarter: technically out of sight really does mean out of
mind, and out of action, in a feng-shui context. If the
client doesn't wish to spend that kind of money, then the

installation of a feng-shui mirror surrounded by the eight trigrams in the Later Heaven Sequence could be expected to deflect some of the trouble. Such mirrors are a common sight in today's Hong Kong and Singapore. More naturally, the planting of trees or the construction of a ming t'ang pond or tank constantly supplied with fresh water might do the trick, as well as aesthetically improving the environment.

Many villages, hamlets or individual houses in southeastern China planted their own tree screens or bamboo groves at the rear of the house, with a miniature ming t'ang pond in front for this very reason. In fact where the land is flat, trees are often substituted for the traditional protective mountain range. This practice is reinforced by similar suggestions in feng-shui books such as the 'Yang Dwelling Classic' which proscribed the planting of trees in front of the house, where the assumed south-facing view was not to be disturbed. Trees were also avidly planted to obscure any free-standing rocks or inauspicious hillocks.

Such trees must be allowed to grow naturally following their own inclinations, without any pruning, cutting or binding. They should be prolific growers and preferably evergreen (to indicate abundant and continual prosperity). It is an odd coincidence that as the yew fits this description, it has come to be a graveyard guardian in both Europe and China.

Like feng-shui walls put up purely to break an inauspicious line of sight, there are groves of specifically designated feng-shui trees which are carefully protected from any indiscriminate wood-gathering.

The tree and pond are in many ways the most natural elements of urban or semi-urban feng-shui practice, both relying on the munificence of the water dragons for their survival. Pine is often picked out for service as a single feng-shui tree, when it is accorded the respect and offerings usually reserved for a *spiritus loci*, so that its feng-shui function may be submerged in a type of tree-worship.

There is therefore much scope for increasing the beneficent ch'i-accumulating abilities of the landscape. It is in fact this premise which led to the creation of the exquisite Zen gardens located round many shrines in China and Japan even today. The manipulation of the existing elements of the landscape into these gardens, where nature is enhanced not uprooted, is a specialized application of feng-shui.

3

Dragon veins: Form School

Clouds emanate from dragons.

I Ching

It is said by the sages of China that neither Heaven nor Earth is complete in itself, and it is left to Man, the mediator between the two, to complete things and bring them to perfection. The Taoist view is that conscious effort (illumined by a knowledge of the working of Heaven and Earth) may, amongst other things, correct the natural outlines of the Earth's surface to a more perfect configuration which will conserve and accumulate ch'i to the mutual benefit of the Earth, Man, and in the long term Heaven. The influence of the weather ch'i and the cycles of the five elements is important, but 'blind' when compared with the ability of Man to utilize to the fullest extent the latent ch'i of his abode, whilst living for his own benefit, and when dead for the benefit of his descendants.

It is inherent in this system of thought that although Heaven directs the life of man, and Earth conditions this direction, by the improvement of an unfavourable natural (Earth) configuration, man may control his own destiny.

In historical times, those with sufficient power or wealth have made such changes, to their own continuing benefit, as they saw it. Hills not quite high enough have been raised, skylines too sharp have been razed. Natural waterways have been diverted to form moats horseshoe in shape, many of which still show up in ordnance survey maps of China or the New Territories of Hong Kong. Straight rivers can be curved or diverted if thought to be dangerous to existing structures. Quarrying can be stopped if it threatens lines of sight, or the bones or veins of an established dragon, legally if necessary.

Given the necessary resources mountains redolent of the fiery and dangerous potency of Mars can be converted into the squarer outlines of Jupiter, whilst visually boring flat plateaux sometimes have mounds raised upon them to add an element of Yang to an all-Yin environment.

The exaggerated style of Chinese landscape artistry will often highlight these features in a manner which is almost unconsciously pedagogic. To analyse a landscape, the feng-shui practitioner (feng-shui hsien-sheng) observes a number of generalized locational rules qualified by interpretations of particular landforms found in the locality under consideration. To determine the location of the dragon's lair the feng-shui hsien-sheng first walks the length of the ridges above the site to be checked, or in the recent past would have been carried by his servants in a sedan chair, looking for the headwaters of any creek or rill which might indicate the flow downwards of the ch'i towards a potential lair or hsüeh.

He may at this point use the compass, orientating its needle so it matches the red north-south line in the base of the needle well so as to determine potential starting points along the ridge or back of the dragon for the flows of ch'i which will eventually come together in the lair which he seeks.

Having dismounted from his sedan chair or located such a point he will quite often, waiting upon the instant for inspiration, launch himself down the slope as fast as he can run, taking no conscious heed of the incline as he plummets precipitously towards the base of the hill. If his career is checked by a hollow the other side of which is sufficient to prevent him from continuing his descent, he will mark the spot and return to the top of the ridge. Here he will select the second rill, or breaking-off point of the ch'i from the back of the dragon, and, following the same procedure, descend as rapidly as his legs will carry him but without prior direction, descending at the same pace till his headlong flight is checked by yet another rise or hollow. This too he will mark, and having made several such descents it is hoped that he will arrive at a common point of intersection. This he will take as the initial potential lair and formally set up the compass here to observe the surrounding landform features. He assumes that, having himself been checked in flight (he being a 'dragon man'), the ch'i will also be checked, pooled and assimilated at this point. His rapid passage down the hillside also has the second happy result of stimulating any such flow of ch'i, although if one looks at the landscape with the cold eye of a geographer one might notice that quite often animal tracks form what are later to become rills and streams, and by clearing the vegetation by the constant passage of their feet, will predispose the feng-shui hsien-sheng to follow and deepen these passages. This technique is called 'riding the dragon'.

The practitioner of feng-shui would say perhaps that the animals follow the natural line of ch'i, rather than the other way around: nevertheless the end result is the same, that having located the confluence of these, he sets up his compass and proceeds to test whether the 'lair' is sound in other respects. It must be a rich vein of ch'i which is not either decaying or moribund.

At this point it is necessary for him to ascertain the exact bearings of each of the major forms in the landscape up to the immediately visible horizon, picking initially upon the major features such as mountain tops, ridges, bends and streams (that is those which are visible from the site). As a general rule those streams which are not visible do not affect the site, although the feng-shui hsien-sheng may in fact check these out to discover the exact direction in which the stream enters or leaves the visible arena.

The sectors of the compass which apply to the main features are then checked, not only for individual auspici- ousness, but for compatibility between themselves. If the initial readings prove favourable then the detailed

Figure 2 Using the feng-shui compass in the Ch'ing dynasty

delineation of the minor aspects, their relationship to the various members of the family employing the feng-shui hsien-sheng and to the time of the year at which it is proposed to build or bury, are further investigated. However, if there should appear to be a major conflict, then either the family will be notified that a secondary site has been discovered or the entire procedure will be repeated to determine the location of another potential hsüeh.

Thereafter if the site has been found to be satisfactory the hsien-sheng will visit it at various times of the day to determine how the shadows impinge one upon the other, even going to the extent of lighting candles or lanterns on outlying spurs to emphasize the shape of their profile, which may not be immediately obvious in full daylight. Each of these shapes will be taken into account according to the complex rules of the Form School in a balanced decision made on the basis of the number of minor adverse points and their interaction with the major favourable indications of the site.

A report put before the employers of the hsien-sheng quite often precipitates the internal family bickering for which feng-shui site selection is infamous. A firm ruling from the head of the family will decide the fate of this site, and whether the feng-shui hsien-sheng is paid a further fee to discover a somewhat more favourable site.

Finally the consultation of the night sky and the actual positions of the constellations on the horizon at that time of the year can either be confirmed directly, or by the use of an ephemeris, the ubiquitous 'Tung Sing'.

The basic rules of the Form School are elaborated upon at great lengths in the standard texts such as those of Yang Yung-Sung. In each case the rules can apply at any level, from the siting of a city to the orientation of a single room, for the same principles are active macrocosmically and microcosmically. In summary, the basic rules are:

1 Buildings, be they tombs or towns, should if possible be constructed on sloping well-drained land. From a prac-

tical point of view, this means the avoidance of badly drained and low-lying areas which may be unhealthy or easily flooded.

2 To the north of the town, village, grove or house, there should be a mountainous shield or screen of trees protecting the site from the malicious influences traditionally emanating from this quarter.

3 The dead should be buried on the south-facing slope of this shield facing the town and the living. It is interesting to note that the Egyptians traditionally buried their dead and built their necropolises to the west of the towns of the living (i.e. in the direction of the sunset) but when constructing pyramids, they always planned to have the entrance on the north side, a piece of information that has guided tomb-robbers for many thousands of years.

4 The entrance to the town or home should always be to the south and should have a clear view of this quarter from which come beneficent influences. Obviously it is not always practicable to site something due north or south, and the shape of the local landform will, of course, modify this, but these are the basic requirements. Quite often the geographical place names in a region, particularly those of hills or prominences, will give valuable details about its feng-shui orientation, and sometimes there are local traditions which can upset the auspicious orientation with as much as 90-degree variance from the traditional rules.

5 The landscape betrays the presence of ch'i in its positive (Yang) form as a dragon, and in its negative (Yin) form as a tiger. The two different ch'i currents in the earth's crust, the one male (positive), the other female (negative), are favourable and unfavourable. These are allegorically called, respectively, the azure dragon and the white tiger. The azure dragon must always be to the left (east), and the white tiger to the right (west) of any site. The dragon and tiger are sometimes compared with the lower and upper portions of a man's arm: in the bend of the arm the favourable site must be looked for, in the angle formed by dragon and tiger, in the very point where the two ch'i currents

cross or copulate. They are most happily placed when they form a complete horseshoe, that is to say where two ridges of hills starting from one point run out to the right and left in a graceful curve, their extremities gently turning inwards towards each other. Such a formation of hills or mountains is the sure index of the presence of a true dragon (see Fig. 3).

A traditional illustration of this is the favourable situation of Canton, which is placed in the angle formed by two chains of hills running in gentle curves towards where they almost meet each other, forming a complete horseshoe. The chain of hills in the east known as the White Clouds represents the dragon, whilst the undulating ground on the other side of the river forms the white tiger. The most favourable site of Canton is therefore the ground near the north gates, whence tiger and dragon are generated. The best side should be hidden 'like a modest virgin, loving retirement'. It is therefore important to look for a recess where the dragon and tiger may mate secretly.

In the classic case of the Ming tombs to the north-west of Peking the actual names of the hills and ranges betray their feng-shui function, so that the hills to the east of the entrance to the valley of the tombs are actually called 'Azure Dragon hill', while those to the west of the entrance are called the 'White Tiger'. The last resting place of the ancestors of the Emperor, he who incarnates Heaven on Earth, should of course be perfectly located.

6 An extension of the dragon-tiger rule is that if these cannot be perfectly found in the site then the generalized conjunction of 'male' and 'female' ground will do almost as well. Boldly rising elevations are called Yang (male), whilst uneven, softly undulating ground is called Yin (or female) ground. On ground where the male characteristics prevail, the best site is on a spot having female characteristics, either visible or indicated by the compass, whilst on a locality which is on the whole female ground, the spot for a grave or house should have some indications of Yang. In each case it should be a spot where there is a transition

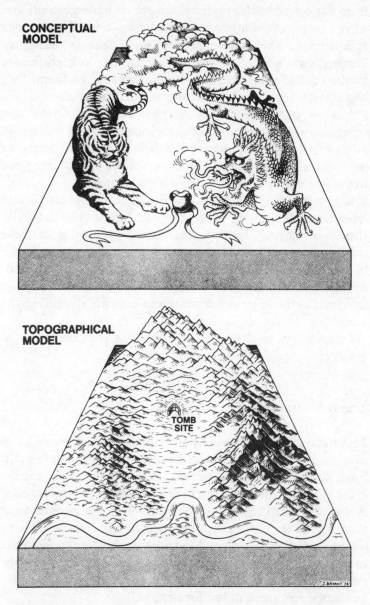

CONCEPTUAL MODEL

TOPOGRAPHICAL MODEL

TOMB SITE

Figure 3 The dragon and the tiger: ideal and real landscape

from male to female, or from female to male ground, and where the surroundings combine both male and female characteristics in the proper proportion – that is male predominating. Where the reverse occurs the indications are totally against the fortuitous accumulation of ch'i, and they will counteract any other favourable configurations.

7 As a consequence of the above it is apparent that completely flat land is not propitious from a feng-shui point of view. In fact where flat land is used for burial or building, artificial mounds or lines of trees are incorporated to the north and/or west sides of the structure.

8 If the land provides a dragon ridge to the east and a tiger formation to the west, the next point that the feng-shui hsien-sheng must consider is the proportion of these two elements of the landscape. The ideal proportion delineated by the Taoists is three-fifths male (Yang) to two-fifths female (Yin), a slightly chauvinistic proportion designed actively to concentrate the benefits of ch'i on the site.

In addition to these orientation rules it is necessary to interpret specific landform manifestations.

Shan, Mountains

Mountains are the traditional abode of the immortals, of dragons and of gods. This is not only because the mountains form almost inaccessible retreats, but because they are the symptomatic crust covering the most powerful dragon veins. A flat landscape (just as in some Western geographical thinking) is an old, tired, worn-down landscape composed of the second-hand silt and detritus washed down from the mountains over the aeons. Mountains, however, are the pristine spring of Yang forces, the most virile and powerful landscape feature, a fit lair for dragons.

The K'un-Lun range of mountains in the far west of China was often considered to be 'the progenitor of all the mountains of the world and the centre of the earth from which the great eastward-flowing rivers of China carry the beneficial influences of the dragon to the coast'.

Consequently the form and structure of all the hills visible to the horizon, with special reference to the shape of their summits, is perhaps the most marked indicator of the Form School. It is therefore one of the first requirements of a feng-shui hsien-sheng that he should be able to tell at a moment's glance which star, planet and element is represented by any given mountain (see Table 3). The rules by which each mountain may be referred to one or other of the five planets are very simply defined by Eitel (1873:57):

If a peak rises up bold and straight, running out into a sharp point, it is identified with Mars and declared to represent the element fire. If the point of a similarly-shaped mountain is broken off and flat but comparatively narrow, it is said to be the embodiment of Jupiter and to represent the element wood. If the top of a mountain forms an extensive plateau, it is the representative of Saturn, and the element earth dwells there. If a mountain runs up high but its peak is softly rounded it is called Venus and represents the element metal. A mountain whose top has the shape of a cupola is looked upon as the representative of Mercury, and the element water rules there.

As a further complication it is necessary to interpret the significance of the cyclical animal of the client's birth date in conjunction with the nature of the prevailing hill form. Thus a person born in the dragon month will be at home with a fire hill, but a person born in a wood month would encounter disaster if he built or was buried within sight of such a hill: the symbolic possibility of conflagration is obvious.

Additionally the signification of all the hills or mountains visible from a particular site should be friendly or at least neutral to each other. As with all Chinese philosophical systems, conflict is to be avoided at all cost. Eitel (1873:58) suggests a classic illustration:

Table 3 The elemental forms of the mountains

Shape	Planet	Element
Conical		fire
	♂ Mars	
Round head, long body		wood
	♃ Jupiter	
Square		earth
	♄ Saturn	
Round, oblong mound		metal
	♀ Venus	
Alive, crooked, moving		water
	☿ Mercury	

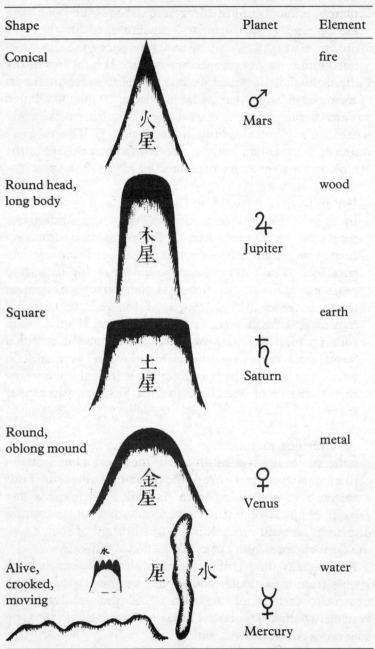

Suppose there is close to a hill resembling Jupiter and therefore representing the element wood, another with the outlines of Mars and corresponding to the element fire, it is manifest that this is a most dangerous conjunction. For instance, the peak of Hong Kong, representing the outlines of Jupiter, is under the influence of wood. Now, at the foot of the peak there is the hill called Taip'ingshan, with the outlines of Mars, and therefore the representative of fire. Now a pile of wood with a fire at the bottom, what is the consequence? Why, it is no wonder that most fires in Hong Kong occur in the Taip'ingshan district.

In addition to the elemental categorization of mountains there is a separate series of mountain forms which owe their influence on the site they surround to the 'Nine Moving Stars'. The Nine Moving Stars are not really 'stars' in any usual sense at all as they have no specific astronomical or astrological locations. They are sometimes called 'fate-categories', 'terrestrial stars' or 'atmospheric stars', and are separate from the standard astrological categories which are woven into feng-shui practice (see Table 4).

Seven of the Nine Moving Stars are sometimes identified with the seven stars of the Great Bear or Dipper constellation (*pe-teu*) which annually rotates around the north polar star. As such they correlate with the seasons of the year. The 'tail' of the constellation at nightfall points to the quarter attributed to the current season, i.e. in spring to the east, or in autumn to the west. They also appear on what is usually the outer ring of the feng-shui compass of the Fukien School. In practice, however, they are used as categories to define the various hill and mountain forms, and thus belong to the Form School of feng-shui.

Although they are given a compass ring to themselves, the Nine Moving Stars are not of central importance to the Compass School, and their details are to be found in the *Han Lung Ching*, 'Classic of the Moving Dragon', by Yang Yün-Sung, the patriarch of the Form School of feng-shui.

Table 4 *The Nine Moving Stars*

The seven stars of the Dipper Chinese name			Meaning	Element	Planet
1	貪狼	T'an-lang	Greedy and Savage (literally covetous wolf)	Wood	Jupiter
2	巨門	Chü-men	Great Gate or Door	Wood	Jupiter
3	祿存	Lu-ts'un	Rank (Salary) Preserved	Earth	Saturn
4	文曲	Wen-ch'u	Civil or Literary Windings (activities)	Water	Mercury
5	廉貞	Lien-chien	Honesty, Purity and Uprightness	Fire	Mars
6	武曲	Wu-ch'u	Military Windings (activities)	Metal	Venus
7	破軍	P'o-chün	Breaker of the Phalanx Broken Army (breaker of luck)	Metal	Venus

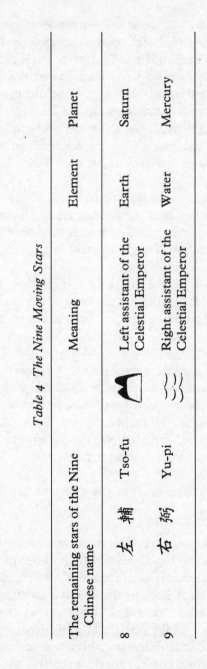

Table 4 The Nine Moving Stars

The remaining stars of the Nine Chinese name			Meaning	Element	Planet
8	左輔	Tso-fu	Left assistant of the Celestial Emperor	Earth	Saturn
9	右弼	Yu-pi	Right assistant of the Celestial Emperor	Water	Mercury

The first seven stars are used by the feng-shui hsien-sheng to indicate influences on the career of a client. They bear a passing resemblance to the five elemental forms of mountains because of their common attribution to the elements, but are much more specific in meaning. For example, the sloping shoulders of the Broken Army (*P'o-chün*) formation would be a disastrous configuration if within sight of the home of a professional soldier, whilst Military Windings (*Wu-ch'u*) would have the opposite effect.

Literary efforts contributing in the Chinese system to advancement in the civil service are enhanced by the presence of a *Wen-ch'u* formation, which might be interpreted as a Water formation if such a career was irrelevant to the client.

There is also a degree of free interpretation based upon the ability of the feng-shui hsien-sheng to interpret the Yang landforms in relation to the circumstances of the client's family: Eitel (1873:58) again provides classic examples:

> For instance, if a hill resembles in its general contour the form of a broad couch, then its influence will make your sons and grandsons die a premature and violent death. If you build on a mountain which resembles a boat turned bottom upwards, your daughters will always be ill, and your sons spend their days in prison.

Eitel also gives an example of the effect of one of the Nine Moving Stars:

> If a mountain reminds one in its general outlines of a bell, whilst at the top there are the outlines of Venus [the P'o-chün formation], such a mountain will cause the seven stars of the Great Bear to throw a deadly light upon you which will render you and all the members of your family childless. Most dangerous are also hills that resemble the one or other of the following objects: a basket, a plough-share, the eye of a horse, a turtle, a terrace, a meadow.

S

向 丁 山 癸

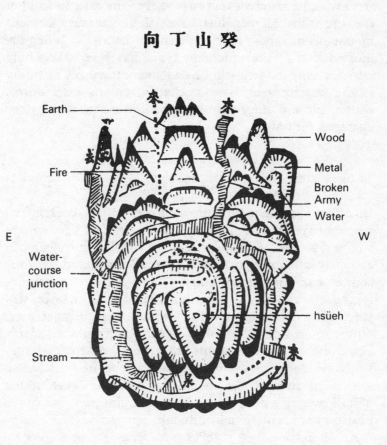

Figure 4 Typical Chinese map of a hsüeh

As a general rule the overly Yin or rounded mountain is not auspicious.

A typical site interpreted according to its hill-shapes might look something like Figure 4. In this the hsüeh or lair is located in the lower (northern) part of the semiperspective map and marked as a small circle enfolded by three rings on either side with an open view to the south (top of the map). Behind the site to the north is the backrest range from which a watercourse progresses to the east. In front of the site (top half of illustration) there are very obvious mountains of almost every type so far described. When the interrelation of the mountain types has been taken fully into account, the feng-shui hsien-sheng turns his attention to the watercourses. The hatched areas are watercourses whose exit and entry points to the site are marked by the character for water.

Shui, Water

In direct opposition to European concepts of orderliness, where a river flowing in a straight line would be a godsend to any engineer or town-planner, his Chinese equivalent will earnestly attempt to introduce 'natural' curves into a water-course at the first opportunity. Quite often even when de-fence is not the objective, a Chinese hydraulic engineer will surround a dwelling or village with a curved moat open on the south side to receive the beneficial ch'i. Such diver-sions of the flow of streams show up in dozens of large-scale ordnance survey maps of areas long under Chinese settlement and provide interesting aesthetic relief in the field. For a rice-growing race, such engineering has never been more than marginally difficult.

An interesting light is thrown on feng-shui principles by a description of a perfect site, or dragon's lair, which reads like the description of a blind spring. It is logical to postu-late that here the dragon is of course in his lair, because it is from here that the water (i.e. the dragon) emanates before crossing the land as a stream, or being evaporated to form (dragon) clouds. (As blind springs are reputed to be discover-able under land marked by megalithic standing stones the hsüeh may be the rough equivalent of an English sacred site, and obviously propitious to live in. Further research on the purely geographical/geological properties of both types of site might prove profitable.)

Apart from their symbolic importance in feng-shui, water-courses are the most immediately recognizable feature of any map. They are also easier to interpret than gradients portrayed either by modern contour lines or traditional Chinese semi-perspective drawings.

Watercourses are the most obvious flowlines of ch'i. In fact the Chinese homonym of the word 'ch'i' means 'stream'. To interpret the feng-shui significance of a watercourse, one must bear in mind the general rule that water flowing fast, or in straight lines, conducts ch'i away from a spot rapidly, and is therefore undesirable; and that slow sinuous deep watercourses, on the other hand, are conducive to the accumulation of ch'i especially if they form a pool in front of the hsüeh under consideration.

As a curved and tortuous course is the best indication of the existence of ch'i concentrations, so the junction of two watercourses is a key dragon point, and if the feng-shui hsien-sheng is using a compass, this 'knot' or junction will be a highly significant and easily aligned point.

While the junction should form a graceful curve rather than a union of conflict, the watercourse so formed should harmoniously cross and re-cross the area in front of the site being assessed, thereby bringing a steady flow of the good things in life without the loss of these resultant upon a rapid and straight egress of the waterway.

Generally stream confluences are beneficial because of the concentration of ch'i, whilst the branching of a stream flowing through course sediment or at the delta of a river is dispersive of ch'i. Sharp bends, like straight lines, are unfavourable, as they act like 'secret arrows' directing demons to the site or destroying or removing the ch'i accumulations. Meanders in the watercourse are much more conductive, as the natural shape of a dragon is that of sinuous meandering.

It is certainly true from a geographical point of view that any watercourse passing through a uniform sediment will automatically meander, so the presence of a straight stream would clearly indicate to both geomancer and geographer an underlying fault in the structure of the land, harmful psychically, as well as revealing at a physical level.

Edkins (1872:75) outlined the rules of streamflow as follows:

> the dragon may be traced to its source. It is observable in the flow of the mountain stream, or in the contour of the earth. The hollow river bed, and the variety of hill and valley are caused by the dragon. Trace the water of a valley to its source. That is the point from which commences the influence that controls human destiny. Water is the element in which the dragon delights. Its winding shape as it meanders through a plain gives evidence of this, for the dragon prefers crooked paths. Since then the dragon gives prosperity, elevates the king and the sage, and is the symbol of all exaltation, social, political or moral, it is all-important to consider the position of water when selecting the site of the grave.

Edkins illustrates this with a traditional example:

> In the valley of the Ming tombs the water flows from the North-west, passes under a bridge in front of the grave of the Emperor Yung-lo, and then pursues its way down towards the plain of Peking on the south east. Hills in horse shoe form embrace the valley. The Feng-shui is good.

Apart from the naturalistic observations of the Form School, the practitioners of the Compass School use the precise points of junction, appearance, disappearance and pooling of a watercourse as sighting lines:

> The chief use of the geomancer's compass is to determine in regard to the water, the direction of flow, the primary source, the points of junction, and the points from which it starts afresh at a new angle.

The configuration of water to the south is particularly important in assessing the potential of the site for wealth-attraction:

> Before a tomb must be running water. Riches and rank flow like water capriciously from one point to another. Hence riches and rank are supposed to depend on the undisturbed flow of the stream which passes under the bridge in front of the site . . . Riches and rank are attached to flowing water, and if due care is taken by the geomancer and by the posterity of the dead, a perpetual stream of worldly honour and wealth may be expected to flow into the possession of the family.

Again, perhaps easier than with mountain shapes, the landscape can be altered by man to improve the feng-shui. Bends can be put in straight river stretches or sharp bends can be rounded (although these are more likely to occur in rocky country and therefore be more difficult).

Even artificial confluences or branches can be created. Preferably the dragon lair or hsüeh should be situated nestled amongst branches of the river rather than directly on the main or trunk watercourse, especially if the main watercourse runs too fast to accumulate ch'i. The more branches, which are the arteries or pulse of the Earth, the more potent the ch'i accumulation.

Water, however, is very necessary in one form or another, for a barren site would indicate a barren offspring, a fate of the first order of evil to a family/progeny-orientated society. A lack of branching or joining watercourses is also to a lesser extent looked upon as having this effect, apart from probably indicating a low local rainfall.

A stream flowing from the east or the west is auspicious if it flows directly towards the hsüeh, deflects around it, and then meanders, for the ch'i brought by the stream enters the hsüeh directly (by a straight stretch of water) but is taken away from the hsüeh indirectly (by a curved path which is slower): it therefore accumulates.

Of course if the water is in the south (forming the traditional ming t'ang or Heaven Pool) it must be calm and still, and if possible the stream entering it, and especially the stream leaving it, should be out of sight of the hsüeh, so that there is no visible loss of the ch'i accumulated by the pool downhill from the hsüeh.

The direction in which the water enters and leaves the pool is useful in computing its feng-shui value, for the Lo-shu diagram of nine squares (with the trigrams) indicates which members of the family are particularly singled out for one fate or another by matching the diagram with the pool's orientation. Details of the relationship of the eight trigrams to the entry and the exit points are to be found in the next chapter.

The 'Water Dragon Classic' (*c.* AD 600) is a specialized manual devoted to the formation of the dragons. Incidentally the dragon referred to without any qualifications in 'Explanation of the Compass', and most other manuals, is a mountain formation dragon. However in the 'Water Dragon Classic' the dragon is the energy and coilings of the surface water flow, a 'water dragon' reflected in the shape of its watercourses.

The 'Water Dragon Classic' classifies watercourses into trunks and branches. The hsüeh should be located among the latter. Feuchtwang (1974:130) summarizes these doctrines:

Water is the path of ch'i and branches, otherwise called inner ch'i 'stop' or may be tapped and are productive, whereas trunks or outer ch'i merely surround the hsüeh. The 'Water Dragon Classic' contains several diagrams showing different types of watercourse formation, indicating with a dot where the hsüeh is, and explaining which are lucky and what each formation signifies. Like the shapes of rocks they too may indicate Elements, animals of the Four Quarters, hsiu constellations and many other things besides. The hsiu [sic, hsüeh] must be at the stomach of the dragon, surrounded by it, just as it should nestle protected at the fork of the mountain ridges.

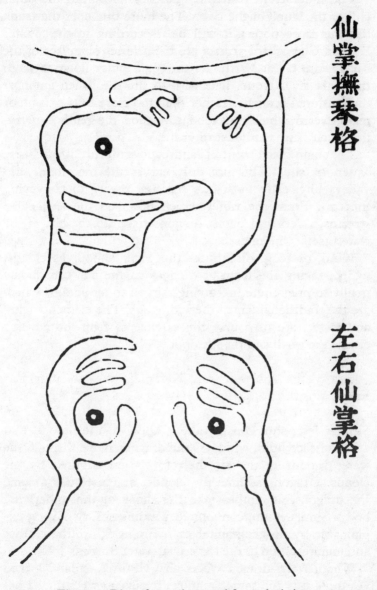

仙掌撫琴格

左右仙掌格

Figure 5 River formations and feng-shui sites

The inner ch'i or stream branches, feed into the outer ch'i or the trunk of the river. The more branches the trunk has the more potent it will be. According to the 'Water Dragon Classic' the trunks are the arteries or pulses of the *Ta Ti*, the Great Earth. As the main pulse flows through the main river trunk, it is wise to site the hsüeh amongst the clustered branches rather than too close to the trunk or main stream, which runs too fast to allow the gentle penetration of ch'i into the house or grave.

The main instrument of landscape sculpture is of course water, or shui. This not only carves the mountains and valleys physically but flows through the earth conveying the ch'i. From the water which flows on the surface in streams, rivers and pools, dragons rise into the air, as the water itself evaporates.

Wind, or feng, distributes the water vapour as clouds, which, taking the form of dragons in the air, consolidate finally to precipitate life-giving rain on to mountains which are the traditional lair of these dragons. The elements wind and water, are of course the essence of feng-shui, which effects the earth and the life on it.

Feng, Wind

Similar feng-shui considerations apply to the flow of that other surface fluid, wind. As the dragons move through the water vapour in the air their forms are adopted by the clouds. Dragons assume the clouds, or the clouds assume the dragons, as clothes take the shape of the underlying body. Similarly the convoluted windings of the rivers, explainable by no geographer or hydrologer, are the clothes and manifestation of the terrestrial water dragons.

Whether the dragon wears airy vestures or land-locked vestures, it is the same creature, for even as Hermes Trismegistus said, 'as above so below', so it is in the Orient where the dragon penetrates both the sky above and the earth below. The form of a dragon is sometimes adopted by the precise curling of a burning joss stick in a draughtless room, a million protean dragon limbs, such as many Chinese mediators must have seen. They knew the forms of feng, the air, long before Western physics crudely formulated the movement of air in terms of convection currents.

Not only is traditional Chinese imagery more picturesque, it is also closer to the tenuous life of the forms of air than any physicist might encapsulate in a formula, no matter how abstruse. The belief that dragons lived in streams or oceans but could fly up to the clouds only to return again to rivers reveals a systematic knowledge of the connection between evaporation, cloud formation, and rain. It is in fact the wind, feng, which carries the dragons of water, shui, aloft to form clouds and thence rain. The falling of the rain effects the landscape by generating patterns in the course of its return to the sea, via the drainage system of rivers which carve the shape of the landscape, eroding valleys, leaving mountain ranges and forming plains. So the very shape of the dragons of earth are conditioned by the 'flight and return' of the watery dragons to their home.

What appeared then to be three different 'types' of dragons can now be seen to be the three interlocking parts of one continuous natural process. The Chinese vision of this is a vision of the breath of life rather than the mechanical version of the geographer who defines the cycle in terms which he can recreate in a sandpit or a laboratory.

Thus dragons, which must not be confused with the European fire-breathing variety which made St George a household word, are the animating essence of the natural system which provided the rice-growing peasant with the essentials for cultivation or the possibility of rapid destruction: truly a beast to be feared.

Dragons are of course not just the animating spirit, but also the very form of the collaboration between feng and shui to raise aloft those exotic forms which clouds often take, which drift inland to release their fertilizing rains on the mountain tops, the traditional home of the Dragon Kings who regulate the whole process. Dragon Kings control the weather, just as they mediate between Heaven and Earth, while the five weather ch'i ply the space between Heaven and Earth: the lightning, rain, wind and sunshine, conveying the effects of the Yang Heaven ch'i to the Yin Earth ch'i.

It is said that if wind has access to a site from all sides, it will scatter the ch'i before it has time to accumulate. If, however, the wind is more mellow, then the vital breath of the earth, ch'i, is retained. There is quite a striking parallel between the flow of air and the flow of ch'i, as wind itself like water is considered to be one of the five weather ch'i which mediate between Heaven and Earth.

It is strange that of all the books on feng-shui, although many mention watercourses (shui), there is very little mention of wind (feng), except by implication, perhaps because of the impermanent nature of this aspect of the earth's surface. There are of course references to hsüeh in hollows protected from strong winds, but not so shielded that the air stagnates. As the dragons of Earth (ti) must be reflected in the dragons of Heaven (t'ien), and as the wind which blows between them represents Man, feng-shui is obviously designed to place Man in the best possible relationship with the dragons of both Heaven and Earth.

4

Time and tides: feng-shui numbers

If a human ruler likes to destroy eggs and nests, the phoenix will not rise. If he likes to drain the waters and take out all the fishes, the dragon will not come. If he likes to kill pregnant animals and murder their young, the unicorn will not appear. If he likes stopping the watercourses and filling up the valleys, the tortoise will not show itself.

Ta Tai Li Chi

Much of what appears to be intuitive reasoning in feng-shui is in fact bounded by the Chinese reverence for law, order and mathematics. A quick glance at the framework of the laws of li which govern the Chinese cosmology provides us with a vocabulary and background to feng-shui terms.

1 Heaven

At the centre of the system is the unity often translated as Heaven (t'ien) impersonal, all-powerful and rather distant.

2 Yang and Yin

T'ien breathes and light (Yang) and dark (Yin) are created. These are represented in the *I Ching* as the whole line (Yang) and broken line (Yin). As the whole line is one thing and the broken line is two things, Yang is equated to one and Yin to two: it follows that all odd numbers are Yang and all even numbers are Yin. Therefore the mating of odd and even numbered ch'i flows are a beneficial combination.

As the ancient literal meaning of Yin implies 'the shady north side of a hill', whilst Yang suggests the 'sunny south side of a hill', immediately you have a direct application to the surface of the earth.

Yin governs the Earth, all that is negative, female, dark, water, soft, cold, deadly or still; whilst Yang governs Heaven and all that is positive, male, light, fiery, hard, warm, living and moving. Of the combination and permutation of the Yang and the Yin is formed the rest of the universe whose life and breath is ch'i.

4 Four Seasons and Animals of the Quarters

In the first chapter we touched briefly upon the orientation of the four quarters. Persisting with the Chinese model in which south is orientated to the top of the page, we can fill in a little more detail by superimposing the four seasons on the quarters. Obviously summer, being the hottest season, is located in the south while the spring is to be found in the place of the rising sun, the east. The remaining seasons face their opposites.

Additionally if we ascribe the full Yang (male) trigram to summer, and the completely Yin (female) trigram to winter we can indicate an increase in Yin from autumn to winter, and a waxing of Yang from spring to summer.

The sun rises in the east, just as the year begins in spring; reaches its peak in the south (midsummer), sets in the west (autumn), and is dark in the north (midwinter). Consequently the seasons are attributed to the four quarters:

Spring – East (equal Yang and Yin)
Summer – South (maximum Yang)

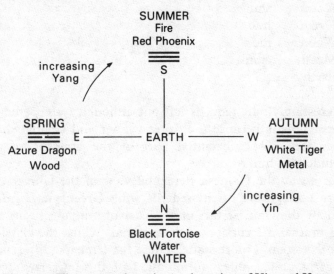

Figure 6 The seasonal waxing and waning of Yin and Yang

Autumn – West (equal Yang and Yin)
Winter – North (maximum Yin)

Further, the five elements of the Chinese can be allocated to the seasons and hence to the compass directions, with Fire going to the red phoenix of summer, and Water to the cold north. The fifth element, Earth, is the odd one out, being located at the centre.

5 The Five Elements – *Wu Hsing*

The Five elements of the Chinese are different from the ancient Greek elements of fire, air, earth and water inasmuch as they include Wood which is organic matter and signifies the whole vegetative cover of the Earth, not just trees, and Metal which symbolizes to a certain extent things fabricated or purified from the Earth.

The Elements are:

Water	shui
Fire	huo
Wood	mu
Metal	chin
Earth	t'u

Interestingly, air, feng, is left out although water, shui, is there. This is because the water vapour and clouds which form the most substantial part of the atmosphere are included in shui.

In a way the Chinese elemental view of the Universe is more ecologically orientated than the Greek view. Additionally the Chinese talk of an order of mutual production and mutual destruction of the elements whilst the classical Greek system is more static. These fundamental differences in early philosophical formulation of the universe reveal two basic differences between Chinese and European culture.

The whole concept of the life and breath, ch'i, of the earth is so obvious to a Chinese but so alien to a European. This early world-view generated separately by each of the two cultures has helped reinforce this difference.

It is a little misleading, however, to refer to these five as 'elements', for hsing indicates movement, so perhaps 'the five moving agents' might be a more appropriate name for the elements. This certainly reinforces the idea that they generate and destroy each other in a continually moving cycle. Like the trigrams and hexagrams of the 'Book of Changes', the *I Ching*, these are also symbols of change and transformation.

The Buddhist concept that the universe is a continually changing panorama of the 'myriad things', in which the activity of change and the Great Absolute behind change are the only constants, provides a backdrop for the theory of the 'five moving agents'.

There are glyphs which explain this interaction in terms of the five elements. Two of the most ancient ones are the *Ho-t'u* and the *Lo-shu*, and these will be examined more closely in connection with the eight trigrams. The first portrays the relationships of the five elements in the Former Heaven Sequence, in their Yang aspect, which is especially applicable to the waxing half of the year. The sequence of the Ho-t'u is thus one of giving birth. The elements give birth to each other in the order shown in Figure 7. Thus Wood burns to produce Fire, which results in ash (or Earth) in which Metal may be found. Metal is also found in the veins of the earth from which (according to Chinese thought) sprang the underground streams (Water) which nourish vegetation and produce Wood.

On the other hand, the Lo-shu portrays the waning half of the year, the Yin aspect. The Later Heaven Sequence of the trigrams indicates the destructive order of the elements. Each element destroys another in the sequence shown in Figure 8, so that in feng-shui theory the destroyer is inimical to the destroyed element.

Both these cycles are more easily appreciated in terms of the wide range of things covered by the 'elements'. Feuchtwang (1974:42) admirably explains it:

Wood is understood to be all vegetation, which is fed by Water, and swallows, covers, binds earth, is cut down by metal implements and ignites; if Water is understood to be all forms of fluid including the liquefication of metal by fire, and which can be solidified by being stanched with earth; and if Earth is understood to mean all mixed, impure, and inanimate substances including the ash produced by fire.

When these five elements are considered in relation to other fields of Chinese thought a wide-ranging set of correspondences is evolved. These form the background to much traditional Chinese philosophy and conjecture and are also part of the unarticulated fivefold associations taken for granted by a practitioner of feng-shui.

Table 5 The five elements according to the Former Heaven
Sequence

ELEMENT	Wood	Fire
DIRECTION	East	South
COLOUR	Blue/green	Red
SEASON	Spring	Summer
NUMBERS AND TEN HEAVENLY STEMS		
(Yin)	8 i	2 ting
(Yang)	3 chia	7 ping
CLIMATE	Windy	Hot
MOUNTAINS	T'ai-shan	Heng-shan (in Hunan)
PLANETS	Jupiter	Mars
ANIMALS	Azure Dragon	Phoenix/ Red Bird
ORIFICES	Eyes	Ears
EMPERORS	Fu-Hsi	Shen-Nung
THEIR ASSISTANTS	Chü Mang	Chu Jung
QUALITIES	Formable	Burning and ascending
FIVE CLASSES OF ANIMAL	Scaly (fishes)	Feathered (birds)
FIVE DOMESTIC ANIMALS	Sheep	Fowl
NUMBER	8	7
YIN/YANG	lesser Yang	greater Yang
WEATHER CH'I	Wind	Heat

Earth	Metal	Water
Centre	West	North
Yellow	White	Black
	Autumn	Winter
10 chi	4 hsin	6 kuei
5 wu	9 keng	1 jen
Humid	Dry	Cold
Sung-shan	Hua-shan	Heng-shan (in Hopei)
Saturn	Venus	Mercury
Ox or Buffalo/ Yellow Dragon	White Tiger	Snake and/or Tortoise/ Dark Warrior
Mouth	Nose	Anus and Vulva
Huang-ti	Shao-hao	Chüan-hsü
Hou-t'u	Ju-shou	Hsüan-ming
Producing edible vegetation	Malleable and changeable	Soaking and descending
Naked (man)	Hairy (mammals)	Shell-covered (invertebrates)
Ox	Dog	Pig
5	9	6
	lesser Yin	greater Yin
Sunshine	Cold	Rain

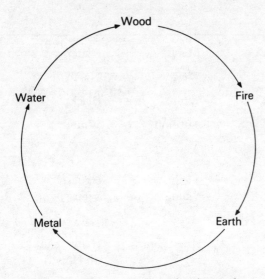

Figure 7 The mutual production order

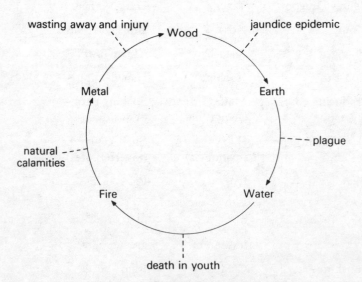

Figure 8 The mutual destruction order

8 *Pa Kua*, The Eight Trigrams of the *I Ching*

The *I Ching* is a binary system of divination derived from the two basic units Yin and Yang, respectively, the female broken line (– –) and the male unbroken line (—).

A trigram is a three-tier combination of Yin and Yang lines: consequently there are 2^3 or eight possible trigrams.

Table 6 The eight trigrams or pa kua

Ch'ien	乾	Heaven, the sky, the celestial sphere	☰
Tui	兌	Watery exhalations, vapours, clouds	☱
Li	離	Fire, heat, the sun, light, lightning	☲
Chên	震	Thunder	☳
Sun	巽	Wind and wood	☴
K'an	坎	Water, rivers, lakes, seas, etc.	☵
Kên	艮	Mountains	☶
K'un	坤	Earth, terrestrial matter	☷

The trigrams are combined one with another to form 8 by 8 combinations, that is 64 hexagrams. The words trigram and hexagram (not to be confused with the Western hexagram or Star of David, which is two interlocking triangles) purely indicate the number of lines in each of these two types of figure. It is the hexagram which is the final product of the *I Ching* divinatory process and which conveys the answer to the question posed.

Each of the hexagrams has a commentary (depending on the configuration of its lines) reputedly written by King Wên and the Duke of Chou in the twelfth century BC, and this forms the bulk of the *I Ching* text.

Most translations of the *I Ching* of necessity place emphasis upon the actual text or the divinatory answers rather than on the meaning of the trigrams and hexagrams themselves. These meanings are given in the so-called 'wings' or later appendices of the *I Ching* reputedly written by Confucius. These 'wings' are much older than the commentaries which often take the majority of the space in current English editions of that great classic. Such phrases in the 'wings' as 'K'an is water, the trigram of due north, where the ten thousand things return' is a specific indication of the relation between this trigram and north in the Later Heaven Sequence.

However, the trigrams are attributed to the points of the compass in two distinct and separate arrangements. These are referred to respectively as the Former Heaven Sequence (allegedly devised by Fu-Hsi and probably the earlier of the two) and the Later Heaven sequence (identified with King Wên, the first ruler of the Chou dynasty). Although the history behind these two arrangements need not concern us, the fact that two arrangements are radically different is important. The two sequences are shown in Figure 9.

The lines of the trigrams closest to the centre of the circle are the lowest lines and, as with the hexagrams, are counted as the first line. Remember also that the south faces the top of the page, and the north the bottom, in line with Chinese practice and the belief that the south was the most beneficent of the compass points and should therefore be at the top. This is possibly a racial memory of the early invasions of China by the later ruling race, which always proceeded towards the south, bringing death and destruction from the north.

Line 1 determines the sex of each trigram, the middle line is the next criterion of relative Yin- or Yangness. The third line (i.e. outermost) is the least crucial. This way a hierarchy can be built up extending from Ch'ien to K'un.

The Former Heaven Sequence is the ideal version, whilst the Later Heaven Sequence is the practical application of the trigrams to the earth. The Former Heaven Sequence is appropriately enough attributable to the Heaven Plate and the Later Heaven Sequence to the Earth Plate on the feng-shui compass. The latter has the more practical application to the strategically important Earth ch'i.

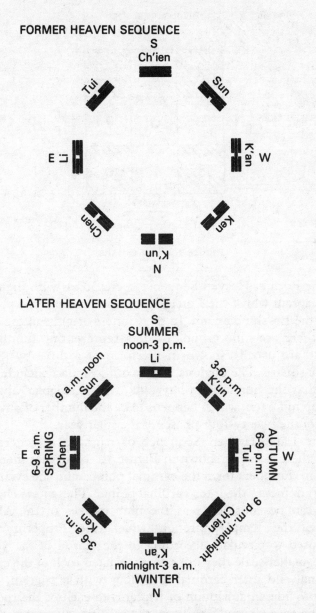

Figure 9 Former Heaven and Later Heaven Sequence of the eight trigrams

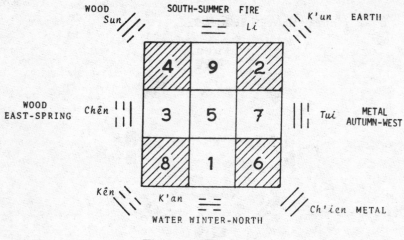

Figure 10 The Lo-shu

The Former Heaven Sequence corresponds with the Ho-t'u diagram whilst the Later Heaven Sequence corresponds with the Lo-shu diagram. In the Chinese original of the Lo-shu there are nine groups of dots representing numbers. These are usually shown in the form of a three by three magic square. The obvious virtues of the square include the fact that the numbers in any rank, file or diagonal always add up to fifteen, which happens to be the number of days in each of the twenty-four phases of the solar year.

The Later Heaven Sequence of trigrams is generated from the Lo-shu as shown in Figure 10. Note that the odd (or Yin) numbers form the cardinal points, and the even (or Yang) numbers the inter-cardinal points. These nine chambers can be considered as the nine palaces of the Ming T'ang, the temple through which the Emperor was supposed to circulate according to the season of the year. On a smaller scale they not only associated each of the eight cardinal and inter-cardinal directions with a trigram, but also provide an ascription of trigrams to each of the rooms of a house or temple built on the traditional square plan, with the central courtyard (square 5) not associated with a specific trigram.

The trigrams thus provide indications of the best rooms
of a house for specific purposes or for specific members of
the family. As each trigram is associated with one or other
member so he is better served if his bedroom is located in
this quarter of the house. On a larger scale trigrams help
determine the most appropriate direction for doorways or
city gates.

When considering a building site the trigrams are also
used to evaluate watercourse entry and exit points. The
book 'Explanations of the Compass' points out that certain
entry and exit points of a watercourse may conflict, for one
is judged by the Former Heaven Sequence and the other by
the Later Heaven Sequence.

If these points of the compass are attributed to the same
trigram (but in different Sequences) then the site is considered inauspicious. Thus the water may enter by the compass
point of the K'un trigram (in one Sequence) and leave by
the K'un direction (according to the other Sequence). The
flow of ch'i which connects a trigram with itself, connects
the two Sequences, and this causes a 'short circuit' between
Heaven and Earth thus rendering the site unusable.

The Later Heaven Sequence is used for the detection of
Yin-Yang harmony or disharmony at particular points,
whereas the Former Heaven Sequence indicates the circular
waxing and waning of Yin and Yang in the archetypal or
heavenly form.

Although the two sequences appear to contradict each
other, the logic of the system is preserved if they are
considered separately, and if it is remembered that the
Former Heaven Sequence stands for the Heavenly order,
whilst the Later Heaven Sequence treats of the less perfect
cycles of seasons, and manifestations on the earth itself and
is thus prominent in the Earth section of the feng-shui compass.

Effectively the Former Heaven Sequence predominates
on the feng-shui compass as it is usually to be found in
trigram form on the second ring of the compass. Conversely,
the sub-cardinal points in what is sometimes the twenty-

ninth ring incorporate the Chinese names for four of the trigrams in the Later Heaven Sequence.

The correspondences of the trigrams illustrate the qualities which may be associated with ch'i entry or exit points at the eight main compass directions.

Ch'ien corresponds to immobility and strength. It represents a horse, the head, the heavenly sphere, a father, a prince, roundness, jade, metal, cold, ice, red colours and the fruit of trees.

K'un represents docility, bovine cattle, the belly, Mother-Earth, cloth, cauldrons, parsimony, a heifer, large carts, figures, a multitude, a handle, black colours, etc.

Chên indicates motion. It represents a dragon, i.e. the animal of the east (in the Later Heaven Sequence). It also indicates the feet, an eldest son, thunder, dark-yellow colours, development, high roads, decision, vehemence, bamboo and rushes.

Sun means penetration, and indicates a fowl, the thighs, an eldest daughter, wood, wind, whiteness, length, height, a backwards and forwards motion, bald-headedness and a broad forehead.

K'an signifies peril, a pig, the ears, the middle son, water, channels and streams, hidden things, alternate straightness and crookedness, a bow, a wheel, anxiety, distress of mind, pain in the ears, a blood-red colour, high spirits, drooping head, a shambling step; finally thieves and strong trees.

Li means beauty and brightness. It represents a pheasant, the bird of the south (in the Later Heaven Sequence), eyes, the middle daughter, the sun, lightning, helmets, spears and swords, a large-bellied man, dryness, turtles, crabs, spiral univalves, mussels and tortoises.

Kên indicates stoppage, a dog, the hands, a youngest son, paths and roads, small rocks, gates, fruits and cucumbers, porters or eunuchs, finger rings, rats and birds with large bills.

Tui means pleasure, a sheep, the mouth, a youngest daughter, spiritist mediums, the tongue, a concubine, and so forth.

For feng-shui the significance of, for example, the relationship between trigrams and family members is of vital importance when considering which member of a family will receive the most benefit by having his or her representative trigram aligned on the main axis of a site under examination.

The symbolic animals are cardinal point indications for the Later Heaven Sequence, just as are the element or seasonal attributions. The use of the last column of Table 7 will become apparent in a later chapter.

Now, as various members of the family from elder son through elder daughter to youngest son and youngest daughter all have an attribution to one particular compass point, the son or daughter whose point has a 'ceasing ch'i' in their quarter at the time of their parents' burial is not going to benefit as much from the feng-shui qualities of the burial as his brothers and sisters and will therefore argue for a stay of proceedings or a change of site till their compass point is better aspected. Of course if it is a big family (that is, one where most compass points are covered by family members) there is never going to be an all-round favourable burial time and place. Sometimes it follows that there looks as though there is never going to be a burial!

As both entry and exit points of the ch'i flow should be considered, the members of the family are distributed according to the Former Heaven Sequence as follows:

S	Ch'ien	Father
N	K'un	Mother
SW	Tui	eldest son
E	Li	middle son
NW	Chen	youngest son
NE	Kên	eldest daughter
W	K'an	middle daughter
SE	Sun	youngest daughter

Table 7 The trigrams according to the Later Heaven Sequence

Later Heaven Sequence compass point	Trigram		Family relationship	Part of the human body	Natural phenomenon	Element	Season	Stem allocation in rings of the feng-shui compass
SW	Ch'ien	☰	Father	Head	Heaven	Metal	Heaven	chia
NW	K'un	☷	Mother	Belly	Earth	Earth	Earth	i
E	Chên	☳	Eldest son	Foot	Thunder	(Wood)	Spring	keng
SE	Sun	☴	Eldest daughter	Thighs	Wind	Wood		kuei
N	K'an	☵	Middle son	Ear	Moon	Water	Winter	hsing
S	Li	☲	Middle daughter	Eye	Sun, lightning	Fire	Summer	jen
NE	Kên	☶	Youngest son	Hand	Mountain	(Wood)		ping
W	Tui	☱	Youngest daughter	Mouth	Lake	(Water and Metal)	Autumn	ting

10 The Ten Heavenly Stems

The ten Heavenly Stems mark the position of the constellations at the beginning of the new year. As their name implies, the ten Heavenly Stems apply to the Heaven Plate on the compass rather than the Earth or Man Plate, though they do occur on the latter.

Stems being connected with water are used by the feng-shui hsien-sheng to estimate the quality of or the breaks, turns, junctions, points of appearance and points of disappearance of watercourses visible from the prospective hsüeh. The Stems are in fact sometimes referred to as 'containing water'. Remember that even in the West the phrase 'milky way' applies to the stars showing an unacknowledged connection between them and water or milk. The Egyptians also saw the stars as the milk from the breasts of Nuit, goddess of the sky.

Table 8 The ten Heavenly Stems

Number and name		Element
1	甲 chia	Wood
2	乙 i	
3	丙 ping	Fire
4	丁 ting	
5	午 wu	Earth
6	己 chi	
7	庚 keng	Metal
8	辛 hsin	
9	壬 jen	Water
10	癸 kuei	

Four of the Stems are considered lucky, and four unlucky.

Unlucky stems	Lucky Stems
1	3
2	4
9	7
10	8

The relative luck of the Stems is related to their association with the trigrams, the unlucky Stems in this case being associated with Ch'ien and K'un trigrams which are unlucky because they are overwhelmingly Yang and Yin respectively with no admixture.

Contrariwise, because Stems 3, 4, 7 and 8 are associated with the Ken and Sun trigrams which have a suitable mixture of Yin and Yang, they are lucky.

Stems 1 and 9 are considered as Yang 'orphans', that is, children left alone in the world who therefore need to extend their own self-reliance in a very Yang way.

Stems 2 and 10 are Yin emptiness: quite the reverse, but again an undesirable state, with no balance of Yang. Again the Chinese desire for moderation and balance asserting itself in the context of their symbology. Orphan-emptiness literally means 'unlucky' in Chinese.

Stems 3 and 7 are Yang prosperity. Here the lucky Stems have a blend of Yang and Yin.

Stems 4 and 8 are Yin assistance. Again a lucky blend. 'Prosperity-assistance' is the Chinese compound word for 'lucky'.

Stems 5 and 6 stand for the centre and do not partake of any particular direction. On the scale of numbers 1 to 10 they also stand at the middle, 5 and 6 being respectively half of the Stems and half of the Branches. They are also allocated to no trigram, as of course there are only eight trigrams to go round ten Stems. They are referred to as the 'Tortoise-shell', a symbol for the middle or the universe. They therefore have no truck with specific ch'i. They may, if anything, be unlucky but they are more correctly thought of as negative rather than unlucky, in that they may be used to control the dispersal of sha (noxious vapours), by imposing the rule of the tortoise on the sha to dispatch it to its proper place. They are almost impartial guardians against sha because they have no specific ch'i attributed to them with which to become involved.

The Stems, like the Branches, also do service in other ways, and often stand for the numerals from 1 to 10, or grouped in Yin-Yang pairs stand for the five elements.

12 The Twelve Earthly Branches

The twelve Earthly Branches are sometimes also referred to as the twelve Horary Branches. The Branches give specific information about time or place. The twelve main points of the compass are those allocated to the twelve Earthly Branches and their basic function is to mark the terrestrial directions. They are basically more at home on the Earth and Man Plates of the compass than the Heaven Plate. They mark the location of earth dragon ch'i.

Taken on their own the Branches also indicate the twelve double-hour divisions of the day as well as the twelve months of the year.

The Branches have come to be used as time markers for anything involving a fraction of twelve, including the Great Year, the duration of Jupiter's revolution round the Sun, of twelve ordinary years.

Hence a year, a month and an hour can all be designated by one of the twelve Earthly Branches, which can then in turn signify a direction of the compass for each of these times providing more mechanics for unifying actions in a space-time continuum. The correlations are shown in Table 9, in which the Branches, although earthly, take some of the animals used as symbols for the hsiu or constellations.

The seasons fit in naturally with the Branches and indicate the best times of the year for initiating projects connected with building or burying. The water solstice occurs

Table 9 The twelve Earthly Branches

12 Earthly Branches	Symbolic animal	Month	Double-hour of the day	Direction
Tzu	Rat	mid-winter	11 p.m. – 1 a.m.	N
Ch'ou	Ox	last-winter	1 a.m. – 3 a.m.	N30°E
Yin	Tiger	first-spring	3 a.m. – 5 a.m.	N60°E
Mao	Hare	mid-spring	5 a.m. – 7 a.m.	E
Ch'en	Dragon	last-spring	7 a.m. – 9 a.m.	S60°E
Ssu	Snake	first-summer	9 a.m. – 11 a.m.	S30°E
Wu	Horse	mid-summer	11 a.m. – 1 p.m.	S
Wei	Sheep	last-summer	1 p.m. – 3 p.m.	S30°W
Shen	Monkey	first-autumn	3 p.m. – 5 p.m.	S60°W
Yu	Cock	mid-autumn	5 p.m. – 7 p.m.	W
Hsü	Dog	last-autumn	7 p.m. – 9 p.m.	N60°W
Hai	Boar	first-winter	9 p.m. – 11 p.m.	N30°W

half-way through Branch *tzu* (due north) which of course is the beginning of the Chinese New Year, and the rest of the Branches follow in order allocating the parts of the compass to the times of the year through *mao* due east (spring), wu due south (mid-summer) and *yu* due west (autumn).

The twelve Earthly Branches are not confined to earth because in interacting with the ten Heavenly Stems they become the sixty sexagenary figures. This admixture of Heaven and Earth produces the set of symbols which bear very directly on Man, the middle term between Heaven and Earth.

60 The Sexagenary Characters

For detailed analysis of the twelve Branches we have to turn to the sexagenary divisions which are each made up of one written character from a Stem and one from a Branch. Thus each Branch is split into five parts, each of which has the character of its Branch plus one of the characters of the five even-numbered Stems (or one of the five odd-numbered Stems for odd-numbered Branches). This way sixty sexagenary character combinations result instead of the 120 which would occur without the limitation of odd with odd and even with even.

Sexagenary characters are also called dragons because they are used to trace the earth ch'i dragon veins flowing through the earth. They also provide the key as to the time of the year at which a particular vein may be 'opened' to the site. Regardless of which compass Ring you use, be it Ring 13, 23 or 31, the attributions of 'lucky' and 'unlucky' to the various sexagenary characters is fairly consistent, there being only minor differences between the Rings (excepting of course where each is on a separate Plate, which gives a 7½-degree divergence in their exact orientation). Of these, exactly half the dragons/sexagenary characters are lucky and half unlucky, with the dragons right on the twenty-four compass points being the luckiest.

Hence for a rough rule of thumb it is best to connect a

site with a ch'i source indicated by a dragon/sexagenary character located exactly on one of the twenty-four main compass points.

Like the twelve Branches, which represent a twelve-year cycle, the sexagenary characters also represent a sixty-year cycle. It is this cycle which provides each Chinese year with its designation of element and animal, like the year of the Wooden Rat or the year of the Metal Dragon. In each case the animal is derived from one of the twelve Branches and the element from one of the five pairs of Stems which go to make up the sexagenary characters. These designations are popular in Chinese astrology and the sexagenary characters of the hour, day, month and year of birth go into the construction of the horoscope.

The Calendar

The calendar subsumes many of the categories so far considered. The ordinary Chinese calendar is both lunar and solar, the moon determining the length of each month but with the year's length governed by the sun. Further, each day is made up of twelve double hours and divided according to the five elements.

The twenty-four phase cycle of the farmer's calendar or solar calendar is used to this day in China. It is divided into eight chieh and sixteen ch'i. Chieh and ch'i are roughly the same, except chieh mark the beginning of one of the eight parts of the year, i.e. the beginning of a season, a solstice, or an equinox. Each of the chieh/ch'i corresponds to 15 degrees of the sun's movement along the ecliptic and is therefore approximately equal to fifteen-sixteen days.

The year is thus divided into twenty-four chieh/ch'i. It is then subdivided into seventy-two hou (three for each chieh/ch'i). This means that each hou is slightly more than five days long, thus providing a useful ritual period.

The twenty-four divisions of the solar calendar are as follows (approximate dates):

CHIEH	Li ch'un	Beginning of Spring	begins 5 Feb.
CH'I	Yu shui	Rain water	begins 20 Feb.
CH'I	Ching chih	Excited insects	begins 7 March
CHIEH	Ch'un fen	Spring Equinox	begins 22 March
CH'I	Ch'ing ming	Clear and bright	begins 6 April
CH'I	Ku yu	Grain rain	begins 21 April
CHIEH	Li hsia	Summer begins	begins 6 May
CH'I	Hsiao man	Grain filling	begins 22 May
CH'I	Mang chung	Grain in ear	begins 7 June
CHIEH	Hsia chih	Summer Solstice	begins 22 June
CH'I	Hsiao shu	Slight heat	begins 8 July
CH'I	Ta shu	Great heat	begins 24 July
CHIEH	Li ch'iu	Autumn begins	begins 8 Aug.
CH'I	Ch'u shu	Limit of heat	begins 24 Aug.
CH'I	Pai lu	White dew	begins 8 Sep.
CHIEH	Ch'iu fen	Autumn Equinox	begins 24 Sep.
CH'I	Han lu	Cold dew	begins 9 Oct.
CH'I	Shuang chiang	Hoar frost descends	begins 24 Oct.
CHIEH	Li tung	Winter begins	begins 8 Nov.
CH'I	Hsiao hsueh	Slight snow	begins 23 Nov.
CH'I	Ta hsueh	Great snow	begins 7 Dec.
CHIEH	Tung chih	Winter Solstice	begins 22 Dec.
CH'I	Hsiao han	Slight cold	begins 6 Jan.
CH'I	Ta han	Great cold	begins 21 Jan.

The twenty-four solar divisions of the year also have spatial equivalents. The compass links them to the twenty-four directional points, and thus it integrates time and space considerations into a single series of symbols. The sexagenary character cycles are based on a twelve-fold division of the circle by the twelve Branches. If the twenty-four points are paired into twelve, each pair contains one Branch and the disposition of Branches is the same in the rings of twenty-four points as it is in the compass rings of sexagenary characters. The sexagenary characters therefore are an elaboration of both the twenty-four points and the twenty-four solar divisions of time. In short feng-shui bridges space and time using the compass to interpret both.

This gives a significance to one particular direction at a particular time of the year. It is for this reason that burial or building is often put off for many months, for although a suitable site may have been found, it is necessary to wait till the time of the year coincides with the site's orientation.

In opposition to the practical farming 'real' solar calendar is the Imperial Calendar which is based on the lunar cycle. The Imperial Calendar or *huang-li* is based upon cycles of sixty days and sixty years, just as sixty and its factors (12 by 5 elements) are crucial divisions of the feng-shui compass.

It is not possible to be as exact with the Chinese months of the Imperial lunar calendar. In order to compare the lunar calendar with the solar calendar you have to insert seven intercalary months in every ten years. When the winter solstice fell near the last day of the eleventh lunar month, an intercalary month was ordained by the Imperial Calendar-makers for the following year. Lunar months were numbered but not named, the twelfth month coming somewhere between January and February.

As the lunar calendar is the sacred calendar, according to which the annual festivals are timed, it is not the calendar of practical use. Farmers use the solar calendar to time the agricultural cycle, as is indicated by the names of the ch'i/chieh periods, and because sexagenary cycles and the lunar calendar are impractical except for use in divination, horoscopes and for keeping historical records.

The lunar calendar, however, provides the base for astrological calculations which link individuals to specific sites. The importance of the personal equation in relation to a particular site is sometimes overlooked. If a feng-shui hsien-sheng is assessing a site for a building project, then he has to know the date and time of birth of the owner. If he is, however, examining a tomb or Yin dwelling he has to know the birth date and death date of the person to be buried. This date is then correlated, using the Chinese almanac, the 'Tung Sing', with the directions of the feng-shui compass to find the correct orientation. The 'Tung Sing' relates the month and year of birth to the Chinese animal symbolic of that month and year, an order which is repeated every twelve years cyclically, the full cycle taking five groups of twelve, i.e. sixty years in all.

These animal symbols are related to the direction of the compass according to the table of the twelve Earthly Branches which also takes into account the time of day most appropriate for initiating any action associated with a particular direction. Conjunctions may be found, in fact, which neutralize such dangers. But if it is not possible to discover them, the family is constrained to adjourn the burial until the almanac assigns another direction as peculiarly auspicious. On the connection between individual horoscopes and feng-shui practice, a short quote from De Groot (1897: 976) gives an excellent example:

These [sexagenary] characters being firmly believed to determine his fate for ever, no burial place can answer to the geomantic requirements if the cyclical characters expressing the year of the birth of the occupant stand in the compass on the lower end of the line which the almanac has decreed as auspicious for the current year and in which, of course, the coffin is to be placed. Suppose, for instance, this line runs from south to north, so that the longitudinal axis of the grave should fall within the segment defined on the compass by the limits of the point [tzu] or the North, as indicated on the [compass] circles [Rings] VI and VIII. If then the dead man has been born in a year denoted by a binomium in which the character [tzu] occurs, his horoscope is deemed to collide with the good influences that flow from south to north and to neutralize their benefits, and no blessings can ever be expected from his grave if it is placed in this direction. Hence its axis must be shifted a little to the right or left, without, however, going beyond the northern quadrant; and if it is feared that the beneficial influences of the auspicious line will in this way be lost, the burial must be postponed. The month, day and hour of the birth of the deceased may cause similar collisions, though they are of a less dangerous nature, such dates forming the less important parts of his horoscope.

120 The 120 *Fen-Chin*

This cycle, which is an extension of the sexagenary characters, is so detailed in its subdivision that it is difficult to show on a diagram. More to the point, even on a compass it is difficult to site a particular feature just using the red thread so that it lies unequivocally on one of the fen-chin unless one has eyes like telescope sights.

It is rather like Western astrology where it is possible to draw up a chart with planetary positions measured in degrees, minutes (one sixtieth of a degree) and even seconds (one sixtieth of a minute) but the slightest error in birth time (be it even ten minutes) will throw the positions of the planets out by a considerable amount.

Likewise in the practice of feng-shui, the idea that one can be as accurate as one fen-chin division, that is 3 degrees, by eye, when trying to sight the top of a mountain five miles away with a bit of thread and two weights, is ludicrous. Consequently at this level of minuteness only the most hawk-eyed *afficionado* can come up with definitive answers. In addition, the compass needle being only an inch or so long is not going to be able to guarantee absolutely the placing of the compass even under the best of conditions.

Accordingly any simplified version of a feng-shui compass would exclude the 120 fen-chin divisions and might be tempted to exclude the sixty sexagenary characters. However if the latter were omitted it becomes difficult to establish whether a specific vein of ch'i is waxing or waning. Thus when a bearing is taken and ascribed to one of the sexagenary characters, the state of the ch'i in that feature of the landscape can be determined and the six-day period of the year appropriate to the feature can also be obtained. If it is decided to connect the influence of the feature being sited to the potential hsüeh, dragon's lair, then the burial or building is not executed till those six days come round. This way a certain vein of ch'i can be tapped from the surrounding landscape above all other veins and this vein continues to supply the hsüeh from thenceforth.

The 120 fen-chin combined the 24 points of the compass, 40 blank spaces, 48 of the sexagenary combinations, and 8 of the stems, into one series. This series contains all of the specifically divinatory associations of the Branches, Stems and compass points.

Last, the category found on the outer rim of most compasses is the twenty-eight unevenly spaced constellations which, as they reflect the night sky, do not dovetail mathematically with any of the other cosmological categories.

28 The Twenty-Eight *Hsiu*

Hsiu literally means 'mansion' and has been applied to the twenty-eight unevenly sized minor constellations by which the sky is divided because the sun, moon and five planets were seen to pass through them, 'residing' in each for a given length of time.

The twenty-eight hsiu are asterisms or minor constellations whose approximate position in the sky and the stars they include are given in Table 10.

The identification of the hsiu was first made about 2400 BC and traditionally they formed a rough belt round the equator. In the course of time they have moved some distance from their former positions but the areas of sky where they used to be located are still referred to as the hsiu. Thus the heavens are divided into twenty-eight uneven-sized segments and on the compass these segments are arrayed in the same order with the centre of the compass doing service as the North Pole. The hsiu are like the twenty-eight Mansions of the Moon of Western astrology.

Some of the animals associated with the hsiu have been appropriated by the twelve Earthly Branches as their particular symbols. These symbols will sometimes coincide with the intuitive interpretations of the Form School of feng-shui who may see a hill shaped like a turtle and refer it to that part of the compass occupied by the constellation

Table 10   The twenty-eight hsiu

1	Chio	Horn
2	K'ang	Neck
3	Ti	Root
4	Fang	Room
5	Hsin	Heart
6	Wei	Tail
7	Chi	Winnowing Basket
8	Nan tou or T'ai tou	Southern Dipper or Great Dipper
9	Niu or Ch'ien niu	Ox or Herd-boy
10	Nü or Hsü nü	Girl or Serving-maid
11	Hsü	Emptiness
12	Wei	Rooftop
13	Shih or Ying shih	House or Encampment
14	Pi or Tung pi	Wall or Eastern Wall
15	K'uei	Legs
16	Lou	Bond
17	Wei	Stomach
18	Mao	(is a graph for a group of stars) the Pleiades
19	Pi	Net
20	Tsui or Tsui chui	Turtle
21	Shen	(is a graph for a group of three stars)
22	Ching or Tung ching	Well or Eastern well
23	Kuei or Yu kuei	Ghosts or Ghost Vehicle
24	Liu	Willow
25	Hsing or Chi hsing	Stars or Seven Stars
26	Chang	Extended Net
27	I	Wings
28	Chen	Chariot Platform

Tsui. A full list of the asterisms and their principal symbols will be found in Table 10.

The allocation of the Branches to the hsiu is complicated by the difficulty of fitting twenty-eight uneven categories of one into twelve even categories of the other. Consequently each Branch, or for that matter each sexagenary character, is spread across an uneven number of degrees of one or more hsiu; not a comfortable fit at all!

Although Eitel refers to the hsiu as signs of the zodiac the correspondence is not that close, because although they do represent certain 'animal stars' there is not obviously such a coherent grouping implied by hsiu as by a zodiacal sign, nor do the animals attributed to the hsiu appear to correspond to particular star patterns.

Besides, the hsiu are measured along the earth's equator not along the ecliptic, as are the signs of the zodiac. The hsiu like the zodiac refers to stars which by the procession of the equinoxes have now moved away from that spot, whilst the hsiu or sign name still persists in being attributed to that part of the sky: this at least they have in common.

The hsiu together with the other cosmological categories considered in this chapter make up the building blocks of the feng-shui compass. An understanding of these makes it possible to understand the compass as a rich indicator of the direction and quality of ch'i flow entering, leaving and affecting a site. When used in conjunction with their temporal meanings, appropriate times can be ascertained for influencing these ch'i flows to benefit the overall energy balance of a site be it a whole town, village, home or single room.

5
Pivot of the four quarters:
Compass School

As to the earth, the east-west direction is the weft and the north-south direction the warp.

Ta Tai Li Chi

Biological work done in the late 1970s indicates that certain bacteria swim in the northern hemisphere northwards and in the southern hemisphere southwards along the lines of the earth's magnetic field. Their inbuilt sensors which respond to the field are in fact made of a form of magnetite: almost 'organic magnets'. Although this was heralded as a new discovery, it was known to the Chinese in the first century of our era. Wang Chung said in the *Lun Heng* (Chapter 52 (ch. 17, p. 4a)): 'So also certain maggots which arise from fish and meat, placed on the ground, move northwards. This is the nature of these maggots. If indeed the "indicator-plant" moved or pointed, that also was its nature given to it by Heaven' (translation Needham, 1962, vol. 4, part 1, p. 262).

Certainly, the Chinese knew of the magnetic effect of the earth's gravitational field on animals, which they possibly attributed to the movement of ch'i through the earth, and so it was a logical development to conclude that the same field affected human beings. Further biological work currently being undertaken does seem in fact to support this theory as more and more members of the animal kingdom have their inbuilt sensitivity to the field discovered. The earliest formal recognition of the effect the earth's field has upon organic life is found in the writings of the Fukien School of feng-shui.

The Fukien School, which is frequently styled the 'house and dwellings method' or the 'method of man', claims as its patriarch Wang Chih (or Wang Kih or Chao-King or Khung-chang, all being variants of his name), and is primarily attached to the use of the feng-shui compass.

The use of the compass for feng-shui purposes probably pre-dated its maritime use, and at any rate had little to do with this parallel development; for the feng-shui hsien-sheng the compass has always been an instrument of the land not the sea. The adoption of the compass by Chinese sailors (*c.* tenth century AD) was in fact probably long retarded by its feng-shui use (beginning *c.* seventh century AD), and by the fact that throughout the Middle Ages, Chinese river and canal traffic predominated over ocean voyages. It was often said that the needle of the feng-shui compass is best fitted for determining the flow of the ch'i in the earth because it has been magnetized by direct contact with earth ch'i in the form of the lodestone, and is therefore able to seek the ch'i out by a kind of sympathetic magic. In about AD 300 the feng-shui master Kuo P'o used the words (translated Needham (1962, vol. 4, part 1:233)): 'The lodestone attracts (literally, "breathes in") iron, and amber collects mustard-seeds. The ch'i (of these things) has an invisible penetratingness, rapidly effecting a mysterious contact, according to the mutual responses of (natural) things.' Such a lodestone or needle will certainly be deflected from true magnetic north by local ferro-nickel deposits, thereby effectively reflecting variations in local geology rather than always being orientated in the same direction.

The Chinese incidentally always thought of the compass as south-pointing, in deference to their use of south as the prime cardinal point. When considering only the cardinal points in relation to the European compass no other difficulty arises except the necessity of viewing the compass as if standing in China with one's back to the north, facing south.

However, when examining the intercardinal points we find that the Chinese divide these by a different arithmetical factor, according to which phenomena are being examined. This means that the Western division of the compass by successive halving of divisions is totally unsatisfactory. The European arrangement produces a division into:

N, S, E, W at intervals of 90 degrees
N, NE, E, at intervals of 45 degrees
N, NNE, NE, ENE, E, at intervals of 22½ degrees
N, N by E, NNE, NE by N, NE, NE by E, ENE, E by N, E at intervals of 11¼ degrees

Now where, for example, the feng-shui practitioner divides the compass by the twelve Earthly Branches, that is at intervals of 30 degrees, it is impossible to indicate which points are meant by using European nomenclature. Edkins (1872) was the first to fall into this trap and found that the orientation of the Twelve Earthly Branches rapidly got out of step with European compass points. Subsequent writers like Feuchtwang (1974) have compounded Edkins's mistake; and Evelyn Lip (1979:19) also applies unevenly spaced European compass points to evenly spaced Chinese compass segments. In addition, while European compass points are just that, Chinese compass bearings refer to a segment of the circle not a specific point on its circumference.

The feng-shui compass is not only divided by twelve but has a number of different 'Rings' divided according to the differing classifications outlined in Chapter 4, with division by eight, twenty-four, sixty and so on, all equally unsuited to description in terms of European compass points. The compass is thus not only a feng-shui aid but almost a pocket guide to Chinese philosophy, astronomy, astrology and cosmology because it contains in its many Rings (up to thirty-eight) a complete summary of all the major categories and divisions of these subjects.

The *Lo P'an*

The compass itself is called the *lo p'an* (or *luopan*) or

occasionally the *chen p'an*. *Lo* means a conch or screw-like shape, a spiral. Loosely applied to the concentric rings of the compass-plate it implies that they radiate out from the centre or Heaven Pool. Sometimes it is referred to as a *ti lo* or 'earth spiral', whilst in the Amoy dialect it was called *lo ching* (or *lo king*) which De Groot translates as 'reticular tissue', as the sectors and concentric circles are reminiscent of a net.

Physically the compass is a circular disc of wood, averaging six to eight inches across and rounded at the bottom like a solid saucer. It is usually set into a square board symbolic of the Earth, which is used when aligning it. The upper surface is divided into concentric circles called *ts'eng* ('stories' or 'layers') and is flat except for the small depression in the centre, the 'Heaven Pool', which contains a magnetized needle, usually less than an inch in length, which has its red end pointing to the south whilst its other end seeks magnetic north. It often has a glass cover. A line drawn on the bottom of the needle-house is aligned with the needle to orientate the compass on a north-south bearing.

The compass is often lacquered or painted yellow on the top surface, black lacquered underneath and inscribed with black and red characters, the whole being varnished to protect it. Such compasses are still available in Hong Kong, Singapore and mainland China, but are quite expensive and difficult to find. The number of rings on the compass varies with the size and cost of the instrument. The reverse side usually has a square-gridded table, and sometimes a guide to the various rings and other notes useful to a feng-shui practitioner.

Although there is much variety, the arrangement of feng-shui compasses follow basically the same pattern, the number of rings varying in the region of 8 to 38. The most comprehensive work on the compass, the *Lo Ching Chieh* by Wu Wang Kang, defines the contents of each ring, beginning at the centre. The various rings incorporate not only consistent sets of symbolism but also other cosmological systems. Some rings are based on a division of $365\frac{1}{4}$ days, some on 360 degrees, others on the 28 hsiu or the 72 dragons. Every numerical division is utilized so that the diviner can judge a particular geomantic situation according to any of the above criteria.

The eight trigrams indicate the cardinal points, and the 'corner' points between them. These are further divided into the twenty-four directional points, which are also used on Chinese mariners' compasses. Beyond this, the compass is divided into 60 points, then 120, and finally 360, the number of degrees in the full circle.

There are other cycles involved as mentioned above, but the main divisions can all be expressed as a multiple of twelve, plus the eight trigrams:

Trigrams	8	
Heavenly Stems	10 =	2 × 5 (the elements)
Earthly Branches	12 =	12 × 1
Directional points	24 =	12 × 2
Sexagenary characters	60 =	12 × 5
Dragons	72 =	12 × 6
Fen-chin	120 =	12 × 10
Degrees in a circle	360 =	12 × 30
Days in a year	$365\frac{1}{4}$ =	implied in 360

The compass is thus firmly based on multiples of twelve, the twelve Earthly Branches, the twelve months of the year and the twelve double hours of the day. The five elements and ten Stems interact with the Branches throughout the whole cycle.

The Diviner's Board (*Shih*)

Needham has an interesting theory possibly explaining the origin of the compass. He suggests that early divining boards were used as fields upon which were thrown the divining instruments. These formed the patterns of the constellations, revealing which constellations were operating on what earthly conditions at any particular moment, much in the manner of casting *I Ching* hexagrams for an estimate of the changes operative at a particular moment. This diviner's board (*shih*) was probably made of bronze or lacquered wood and consisted of a round plate representing the heavens mounted above a square board symbolizing the earth. This model of the cosmos was marked with astronomical signs and symbols to represent the days, months and years.

In the centre of the 'Heaven Plate' was a drawing of the Great Bear constellation (often called the Big Dipper, part of Ursa Major which is the most conspicuous constellation in the northern sky). In the divination process, the court magicians would turn the 'Heaven Plate' on its axis in imitation of the movement of the Great Bear's tail around the horizon according to the seasons. Later, the drawing of the Great Bear was perhaps replaced by an actual dipper or spoon made of wood, stone or pottery, and modelled in the shape of the Great Bear constellation. Around AD 100 natural magnetite (lodestone) with its unique properties came to be used for the spoon, and it was found that it turned round to face the same point in the sky, no matter which way the board was turned. As the spoon rotated on the bronze plate, the handle, regarded as the pointer, indicated the south. The Chinese characters used today for the word 'compass' mean 'pointing south needle'.

Needham (1962, vol. 4, part 1, pp. 262–3) describes the diviner's board as:

> composed of two boards or plates, the lower one being square (to symbolise the earth, hence called the ti p'an); and the upper one being round (to symbolise heaven, hence called the t'ien p'an). The latter revolved on a central pivot and had engraved upon it the 24 compass-points, composed, just as in the later traditional compass, of the denary and duodenary cyclical characters, wu and chi (which symbolised the earth) being repeated in order

to make up the full number. It always bore, engraved at the centre, a representation of the Great Bear. The 'ground-plate' was marked all about its edge with the names of the 28 hsiu (equatorial divisions or constellations), and the 24 directions were repeated along its inner gradations. Moreover, it carried the eight chief kua (trigrams) arranged according to the Hou T'ien system so that Chhien [Ch'ien] occupied the north-west and K'un the south-east. This ... differs from that found on all later geomantic compasses where Chhien [Ch'ien] is the south and K'un the north.

It has also been possible to determine what the board was made of as Needham continues (op. cit., p. 265):

Something is known of the wood from which the shih were usually made in later times. The 'Thang Liu Tien' ('Institutions of the Thang Dynasty') from between [AD] + 713 and + 755 states that the round 'heaven-plate' was made of maple wood, and the square 'ground-plate' of selected jujube wood. It may be significant that a particularly hard wood was chosen for the lower board, for that would be the surface on which the spoon would have to rotate if, as Wang Chen-To suggests, the upper board was removed and the spoon substituted for it.

Because of the frictional drag of the magnetic spoon on the Earth Plate, the next development was to insert the magnetite into a piece of wood shaped like a fish with pointed ends and float it or balance it on a pin. Then, when the Chinese learned how to induce or transfer magnetism from magnetite to pieces of iron, they began to make the pointer in the shape of iron fish, tadpoles, and eventually (possibly as early as the fourth century AD) needles. The use of the needle enabled much greater precision in reading.

In all probability, from the beginning of its use at sea,

sometime between 850 and 1050, the compass was a magnetized needle floating on water in a small cup. Among the
oldest types which have been found are flat bronze plates
six inches or less in diameter with a bowl-shaped depression
in the centre where the needle floated. Chinese navigators
remained faithful to floating compasses of one kind or
another until the last part of the sixteenth century when the
dry-pivoted compass was re-introduced with an attached
compass card showing European directions, introduced to
East Asia by Dutch or Portuguese ships.

The proof of the primacy of the compass as a feng-shui
tool before becoming a maritime aid is to be found in a
manuscript which contains a liturgical form for use in the
ship's chapel or before the compass at the beginning of a
voyage. The litany incorporates as saints and sages the
names of a number of feng-shui hsien-sheng both legendary
and real. These include Ch'ing-Wu Tzu (the Blue Raven
Master), Pai Ho Tzu (the White Crane Master), and Yang
Chiu-P'in (perhaps another name for Yang Yün-Sung).

In an introduction written by Li Yü-Hêng in 1570 for
Ch'ing-Wu Tzu's classic he confirmed the change from floating to dry-pivoted compass:

> The needle floating on water and giving the north and
> south directions, is ordinarily called the Wet Compass
> (shui lo ching). In the Chia-Ch'ing reign-period (1522–
> 66) there were attacks of Japanese pirates (on the coast),
> so from that time onwards Japanese methods began to be
> used. Thus the needle was placed in the compass box,
> and a paper was stuck on to it carrying all the directions,
> so that no matter what direction is taken the tzu (north)
> and wu (south) signs are always situated at the north and
> south. This is called the Dry Compass (han lo ching).

It seems altogether possible that the diviner's board was
in fact the forerunner of the feng-shui compass with its
square Earth base into which the circular disc is set. At the
same time the lodestone spoon-shaped representation of the

Great Bear has become the fine needle used by feng-shui hsien-sheng, mariners and geographers alike. Feng-shui was thus the mother of the systematic use of magnetism, navigation and geography, just as astrology was of astronomy, and alchemy of chemistry.

Although modern commentators refer to three groups of concentric circles (or compass Plates as the inner and outer Heaven Plate and the Earth Plate) as integral parts of the circular part of the compass, it is much more likely that the Earth Plate was originally the square compass holder, whilst the separate sets of rings upon the circular part were the inner and outer Heaven Plates.

Needham's suggestion that the divinatory compass derived from the early divining board or shih further confirms the above, in that the early shihs were probably two separate pieces, one circular board placed upon a square board, with the lodestone spoon (or direction finder) on top of the circular piece. It is only one short step from this to inserting the circular disc into the square disc so that it still rotates and has freedom of movement. This would also explain why with such compasses the only alignment marks on the square disc are corner marks rather than the four quarters which one would expect if the circular disc was intended to be fixed rather than rotated according to circumstances.

Therefore, the inner circles, whose alignment is that of the correct needle or astronomical north, are used solely in conjunction with the alignment of the square compass holder, whilst the middle region and outer region of the compass disc, respectively the inner and outer Heaven Plate (deviating to the west and the east of the correct needle), refer to the incoming and outgoing 'breaths' or ch'i flows affecting the site. Thus we have the correct needle and the inner Rings of the compass interpreting any variation of alignment of the building under consideration from astronomical north, whilst the staggered Rings on the rest of the compass indicate movements of ch'i through the observable orientation of the site. This means that there is not just a 'theological' difference between the Plates, but each Plate is specifically used for a different purpose. It might even have been the case that the two Heaven Plates were used, one for Yang dwellings (houses) and the other one for Yin dwellings (tombs and graves), in which case it is likely that the outer Heaven Plate was used for the siting of tombs, with the inner Heaven Plate used for the siting of dwellings for the living.

The Structure of the Compass

Although this derivation is not proven beyond all doubt, it is a useful starting point in examining the structure and development of the compass. On the diviner's board or shih the important facets were the eight trigrams (pa kua), the twenty-four azimuthal directional compass points and the twenty-eight hsiu. Taking these three catagories and working from the centre of the compass outwards we find that almost every compass has the eight trigrams of the 'I Ching' as its inmost ring. If one uses the analogy of the growth of tree rings, then this is probably the oldest stratum. Certainly the eight trigrams appear by themselves in many octagonal or circular Chinese motifs, from the earliest times.

The Plates

Now if either the ideal compass of Wu Wang Kang, or the compass used as an example in the next chapter is closely scrutinized, it will be seen that the next set of symbols, the twenty-four azimuthal directional points, are repeated on at least three Rings. However, the three are 'staggered', the innermost occurrence (the fourth Ring in our example) has its south point at the correct astronomical bearing, while the next occurrence (the seventh Ring in our example) is $7\frac{1}{2}$ degrees west of north, and the third occurrence (the ninth Ring) is $7\frac{1}{2}$ degrees east of north of the first occurrence.

It is not immediately obvious why three sets of identical Rings are needed, each $7\frac{1}{2}$ degrees out of phase with its fellows, but as each of these important Rings has a group of consistent and associated Rings attached, it has become conventional to refer to these groups of Rings as 'Plates'. All but the earliest or simplest compasses have these three Plates.

The hsiu and day/degree Rings

Beyond the eight trigrams and the three Plates come the unevenly divided Rings which contain the five elements spaced erratically (Ring 13) and the 28 hsiu or constellations (Ring 16). The latter almost always form the outer-most Ring, are of variable angular length, and have been detailed at some length in Chapter 4.

Just inside them are often to be found several associated Rings with a complete breakdown of all the 360 degrees of the circle (post-Jesuit influenced) or of the 365 days of the year (on earlier compasses). In the more complex compasses, such as that of Wu Wang Kang, these Rings sometimes appear in other places on the compass face, but in most compasses they occupy the outermost position. In the case of the Ring of 360, this marks off the exact angular length of each hsiu. In the case of 365 divisions a good or bad luck marking is incorporated allowing an evaluation of the feng-shui quality of any direction in relation to every day of the year.

Classification of the Rings

In the compass considered later in this chapter (which has a total of 16 Rings) the Plates divide as shown in Table 11.

In the compass of Wu Wang Kang described in his *Lo Ching Chieh* the Plate system is obscured by the proliferation of categories. It is for this reason that the far simpler sixteen-ring compass illustrated by De Groot (1897, vol. 3, p. 952) is dissected later in this chapter.

Table 11 *The division of the Rings into Plates*

Conventional divisions of the Rings	16 Rings
Eight trigrams	1– 3
Earth group or Plate	4– 6
Man (or Inner Heaven) Plate	7– 8
(Outer) Heaven Plate	9–12
Uneven divisions	13
Table of days or degrees	14–15
Hsiu	16

Evolution of the Plates

According to tradition, the twenty-four azimuthal compass directions were established in their present form at least by the time of Ch'iu Yen-Han, a geomancer who flourished AD 713–41. They were aligned to the astronomical north-south axis and formed the inner or Earth Plate of the compass, whose indicator was the *Chêng Chen* or 'correct needle'.

It seems likely that the central Rings related to the eight trigrams (pa kua) plus the first set of twenty-four directional points, and formed the original core and totality of early compasses. In fact the Chinese maritime compass, which was derived from the feng-shui compass, has to this day this simple form.

In about AD 880 the great patriarch Yang Yün-Sung added the Outer Heaven Plate or Fêng Chen (not to be confused with the 120 fen-chin). Fêng Chen literally translates as 'seam needle' and this Plate is deflected $7\frac{1}{2}$ degrees east of north (or from the Chinese point of view west of south, which amounts to the same thing). When discussing the 'seam needle' Needham incorrectly refers to it (1962, vol. 4, p. 304) as 'magnetic north and south points', which of course it is not, being neither deflected to the same degree as the compass declination at the era of its inception, nor even in the same direction as current magnetic declination. Not only is it incorrect to refer to the 'seam needle' as magnetic north and south (then or now) it is also misleading in that it predisposes the reader to accept Needham's hypothesis concerning its introduction, a rationale which is not to be found in any of the explicit Chinese feng-shui texts contemporary with its invention.

A clue to the reason behind the name 'seam needle' is to be found in a discussion of steel needles in T'ao Ku's tenth-century *Ch'ing I Lu* (ch. 2, p. 23b) which states that, 'Seamstresses or medical men will tell you the merits and disadvantages of different kinds of needles in just as much detail as Confucian scholars talking about brush pens.' Perhaps Yang Yün-Sung labelled his new arrangement the 'seam needle' to impress upon his contemporaries its merit.

Again in the twelfth century a third feng-shui master introduced the third Plate which he referred to as the Chung Chen or 'central needle', this time deviating $7\frac{1}{2}$ degrees west of north from the first or 'correct needle'. It appears that this third addition was called the 'central needle' because it is usually rather ignominiously sandwiched between the 'correct needle' and the 'seam needle'. In fact the central pointing needle is the 'correct needle' with the other two deviating from it. If we take a slice through the compass we get Figure 11. This cross-section shows the relative positions of one of the twenty-four directional points over each of the three Plates. In this example *wu*, the south point, has been chosen to illustrate the angular divergence of the three Plates. It is interesting that the 'central' needle is relatively unimportant in terms of associated Rings.

There is of course only one physical needle per compass, but it is referred to by one of its three possible titles, 'correct', 'seam' or 'central', according to the Ring being read at that time. Table 12 summarizes the outward growth of the compass so far.

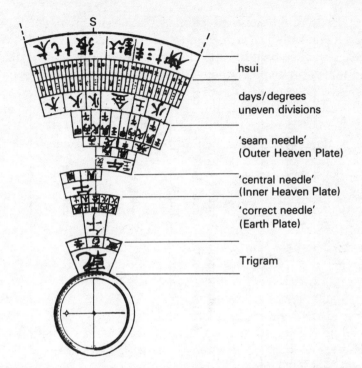

hsui

days/degrees
uneven divisions

'seam needle'
(Outer Heaven Plate)

'central needle'
(Inner Heaven Plate)

'correct needle'
(Earth Plate)

Trigram

Figure 11 The relative alignment of the south point on the three
Plates

Reason for the three Plates

De Groot (1897, vol. 3:967) suggests that the other Plates
were instituted to 'improve accuracy of measurement', a
contention which can be dismissed by simply applying a
protractor to any compass which will demonstrate that the
sector measured by the 'correct needle' of 360/24 = 15
degrees is widened to a possible 30 degrees by the addition
of the other two Plates. Needham (1962, vol. 4:299) is of
the opinion that each of these Plates was introduced in
response to changes of declination over time, and produces
figures in an attempt to corroborate this. However, his
figures (1962, vol. 4:310) are of varying reliability and
are taken geographically from all over China, where the

Table 12 Development of the Rings of the compass

Conventional divisions of the Rings	Needle and meaning	Declination	Established by	Date
Trigrams				Ancient
Earth Plate	Chêng Chen – 'correct needle'	astrononomical north-south	before Ch'iu Yen-Han	before eighth century
Man (or Inner Heaven) Plate	Chung Chen – 'central needle'	7½ degrees W of N	Lai Wên-Chün	twelfth century
(Outer) Heaven Plate	Fêng Chen – 'seam needle'	7½ degrees E of N	Yang Yün-Sung	ninth century
Uneven divisions Table of 365 days or 360 degrees			Jesuit influence	sixteenth century
Hsiu				Ancient

declination would vary anyway, even if all readings were taken in the same year.

I think it unlikely that with widely fluctuating declinations both over time and in space, not to mention local outcrops of rocks which produce wide magnetic fluctuation, two sages should have hit upon the idea of creating new Plates exactly $7\frac{1}{2}$ degrees out of step with the original configuration, especially as at the time Yang Yün-Sung proposed the 'seam needle' variation of $7\frac{1}{2}$ degrees E of N, the actual observed declination was about twice this. Besides the idea of a fluctuation in declination over time was only consciously formulated during the Ming dynasty over 800 years after Yang Yün-Sung's time.

However, a passage from Wu T'ien Hung's *Lo Ching Chih Nan P'o Wu Chi* ('A South-pointer to Disperse the Fog about the Compass'), dating from the sixteenth century, throws an unexpected light on the problem:

Master Ch'iu (Yen-Han) got (his knowledge of the Chêng Chen from) Thai I Lao Jen ... (but) there is also a 'Heaven-measurement' (t'ien chi) and an 'Earth-record' (ti chi). The Fên-chin divisions are arranged in three (Rings), so that although for the earth one follows the Chêng Chen ('correct needle') as everyone knows; in the north (the needle) declined to the NE, and in the south it declined to the SW. Therefore Master Yang (Yün-Sung) added the Fêng Chen ('seam needle'). But in the 'Heaven-measurement,' the needle in the north declined to the NW, and in the south it declined to the SE. Therefore Master Lai (Wên-Chün) added the Chung Chen ('central needle').

As well as confirming the authorship of the two later Plates, Wu T'ien-Hung makes it clear that the reason for the later Plates was functional, not a response to a change in declination over either time or space. It is not coincidental that both Plates should vary exactly $7\frac{1}{2}$ degrees from the original and still acknowledged 'correct needle' because $7\frac{1}{2}$

degrees is exactly half of one of the twenty-four azimuthal direction points which form the basis of the Ring system. Wu T'ien-Hung says that 'for Earth one follows the Chêng Chen ("correct needle") as everyone knows', implying that the Inner Ring was commonly used to determine the Earth directions, whilst the other Rings are for more specialized or esoteric applications. This is a functional, not an historic, distinction. The Plates reflect the Chinese insistence on the interaction of the three levels of Earth, Man and Heaven, where the main divisions of each Ring are reflected in the other. The effect each has upon the other is the basic rationale of feng-shui, which hopes to divine the parallels, and allow man to effect changes in both Heaven and Earth, and their influence upon himself.

Twenty-four azimuthal direction points

The key to the function of each Plate is to be found in the twenty-four azimuthal directions which form their basis. These are not an internally consistent set of symbols, but are formed from three other groups of symbols, used alternatively:

4 of the 8 trigrams used as inter-cardinal points
8 of the 10 Heavenly Stems (omitting the two Earth Stems)
12 Earthly Branches

These are evenly disposed on the compass as shown in Table 13. The table shows that the twenty-four directions divide the circle into segments of 15 degrees. The duodenary cycle of chih characters, the Earthly Branches, is fully represented, but the denary cycle of kan characters, or Heavenly Stems, has lost wu and chi, symbolizing Earth. This omission leaves four places, which are filled by the four most important kua or trigrams.

This is clearly described in Yang Yün-Sung's *Ch'ing Nang Ao Chih* ('Mysterious Principles of the Blue Bag, i.e.

Table 13 The twenty-four azimuthal compass directions

Direction	Earthly Branches (Chih) 支	Inter-cardinal trigrams (Kua) 卦	Heavenly Stems (Kan) 干
N	子 tzu		
N 15°E			癸 kuei
N 30°E	丑 ch'ou		
NE		艮 ken	
N 60°E	寅 yin		
N 75°E			甲 chia
E	卯 mao		
S 75°E			
S 60°E	辰 ch'en		乙 i
SE		巽 sun	
S 30°E	巳 ssu		
S 15°E			丙 ping
S	午 wu		
S 15°W			丁 ting
S 30°W	未 wei		
SW		坤 k'un	
S 60°W	申 shen		
S 75°W			庚 keng
W	酉 yu		
N 75°W			辛 hsin
N 60°W	戌 hsu		
NW		乾 ch'ien	
N 30°W	亥 hai		
N 15°W			壬 jen

the Universe'). The omission may have been essentially practical, since wu and chi would so readily be confused with hsü and ssu, but it is more likely that as wu and chi symbolized the element Earth, which was associated with the Centre, their symbols were accordingly hardly suitable for peripheral azimuthal points.

These basic twenty-four points would have been sufficient for the basis of a single Plate compass, and also for all subsequent mariner's compasses. In fact Chinese navigators reduced the compass they inherited from feng-shui to its simplest form, using only the twenty-four points dividing the compass into segments of 15 degrees each.

The characters used on the compass are not the characters commonly used in China to represent directions. Their origin or etymology is, for the most part, lost in the mists of antiquity, but many of them date back over 4,000 years when they appeared on early oracle bones. The twelve Earthly Branches are also associated with symbolic animals which compose the Chinese zodiac. Each of these creatures is supposed to exercise an astrological influence over a particular two-hour period of the day, and one year out of every twelve.

The relationship between the feng-shui and maritime use of the compass is illuminated by the *Chiu T'ien Hsüan Nü Ch'ing-nang Hai-chiao Ching* ('The Nine Heavens Mysterious Girl's Universe [lit. 'blue bag'] and Sea Corner Classic'), commonly attributed to Kuo P'o (AD 276–324), but in fact probably dating from soon after Yang Yün-Sung. The title, which has been variously translated, is interesting because it refers to the Universe as the 'blue bag', an indication of strong Taoist associations, and to the 'sea angle' or 'ocean corner', probably indicating either the 'new' maritime use for the compass or suggesting its ability to seek out a flow of water from any corner of the earth.

The 'mysterious girl' of the title, Hsüan Nü, 'in the daytime ... determined the directions (of the compass) by the rising and setting of the sun. In the night she determined the directions by the divisions of the hsiu', or in other words, she behaved just as sailors have for centuries. However, with the invention of the 'south-pointer', 'a copper plate was made with exactly 24 azimuth points (chosen

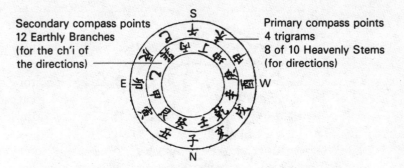

Figure 12a The primary and secondary compass points

from) the ten Heavenly Stems (which had been associated with the) Heaven-plate (t'ien p'an) (of the Han dynasty diviner's board or shih), and the twelve Earthly Branches (which had been associated with the) Earth-plate (ti p'an) (of the diviner's board).' The former are called li hsiang na shui and the latter ko lung shou sha.

An earlier passage reveals why different sets of symbols are used to make up the twenty-four compass points by 'using the ten Heavenly Stems (t'ien kan) for the directions (fang so), and the twelve Earthly Branches (ti chih) for the ch'i the directions (fang ch'i)'. This also explains why the twenty-four points are divided into primary and secondary points. The centre of the accompanying diagram shows clearly the distinction between them (Figure 12a). These two Rings are summarized in a Ring carrying all twenty-four points and aligned (with South at top) according to the 'correct needle' (astronomical north-south) (Figure 12b).

The *Hai Chio Ching* explains that 'nowadays feng-shui practitioners use the Chêng Chen ("correct needle") and the Heaven-plate denary azimuth points to find out where the dragon (ko lung) is.' Thus the 'correct needle' was used to locate the dragon, with the Stems and trigrams indicating the directions, while the Earthly Branches indicated the ch'i of the directions, or the dragons.

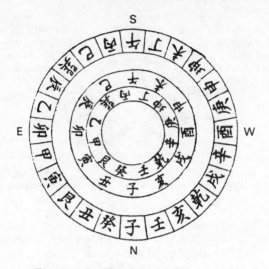

Figure 12b The full 'correct needle'

Introduction of the 'seam needle'

Having established the two aspects of the basic twenty-four 'correct needle' compass points, in which every second point indicates direction and every other point indicates a potential dragon, it is obvious that the compass needs a second ring of points staggered half a division to the left or right to give a 'round the clock' indication of potential ch'i flows. No natural landscape is going to be formed so that potential ch'i sources occur only at every second compass point, so by staggering the points half a division, every feature on the horizon can have a corresponding compass ch'i reading.

It is for this reason that a second Ring is a necessary part of the feng-shui lo p'an. As the *Hai Chio Ching* probably dates from shortly after the introduction of the 'seam needle' (Fêng Chen), the latter is shown on the illustration (Figure 12c). It is significant that according to the *Hai Chio Ching*, feng-shui adepts use the Chêng Chen ('correct needle') to 'find out where the dragon is, (but) they use the Fêng Chen

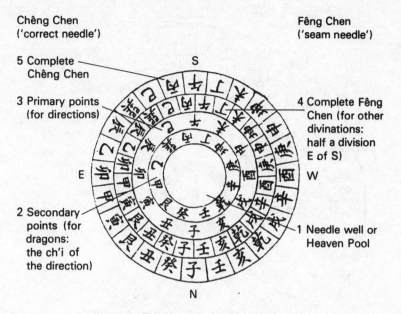

Chêng Chen
('correct needle')

Fêng Chen
('seam needle')

5 Complete Chêng Chen

3 Primary points (for directions)

4 Complete Fêng Chen (for other divinations: half a division E of S)

2 Secondary points (for dragons: the ch'i of the direction)

1 Needle well or Heaven Pool

S

E

W

N

Figure 12c The 'correct' and 'seam' needles

("seam needle") to perform other divinations (li chan)'. The complete illustration now becomes that shown in Figure 12c. The Rings are numbered in the traditional Chinese fashion with the central needle well counting as Ring 1.

A basic lo p'an

This basic ring layout can be expanded to make a basic lo p'an which might well be found in use today. The example that is shown in Figure 13 dates from the nineteenth century and was copied by the Jesuit Henry Doré in his *Researches into Chinese Superstition* (1914–33).

Few compasses are simplified to this extent. The average compass has more like 16–20 Rings, though less than the full prescriptive 38 of the *Lo-ching Chieh*.

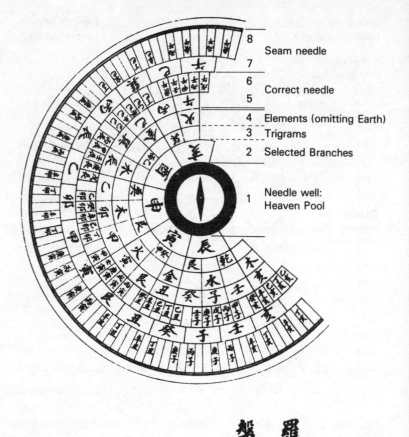

8 Seam needle
7
6 Correct needle
5
4 Elements (omitting Earth)
3 Trigrams
2 Selected Branches

1 Needle well:
Heaven Pool

盤　羅

Figure 13 A simple lo p'an

You will notice that even at this level of sophistication the 'correct needle' and 'seam needle' are sufficient and the 'central needle' plays no part in its construction. Numbering the Rings 1–8 (Ring 1, the needle well), we can identify in Ring 2 eight of the Earthly Branches. Ring 3 contains twenty-four divisions with every other one containing a trigram, and Ring 4 fills the twelve omissions of the previous Ring with three repetitions of each of the five elements, with the omission of Earth. At Rings 5 and 6 we reach the familiar 'correct needle', with the latter Ring providing an amplification of the twelve Earthly Branches. Thus each Branch, or ch'i indication, is divided into five sub-sections, by pairing it with five other symbols. The rationale behind this will be examined later in this chapter.

In Rings 7 and 8 we reach the 'seam needle' and again the same Branches are subdivided, this time into four types of ch'i spaced in a different fashion to the 'correct needle'. This means that each of the twelve Earthly Branches (repeated on two Rings) measure nine different types of ch'i over an angular range of slightly more than 30 degrees, allowing for an overlap of a degree or so between the extremes of each Branch.

By introducing the 'seam needle' the whole 12 by 30 degrees or 360 degrees is encompassed by specific ch'i readings. If you look closely at the tzu or north point you can see that any given degree in the sector it covers might have one or two ch'i readings, but that without the 'seam needle' some parts of the segment would have no ch'i evaluation; an observation which points again to the functional nature of the 'seam needle', rather than to a genesis in the happenstance of fluctuating declinations.

Thus the lo p'an in Figure 13 is quite adequate for the determination of dragons and ch'i flows. On a larger lo p'an the third Plate comes into play.

The 'Central Needle'

Except for an angular displacement of 15 degrees the 'central needle' is exactly the same as the first two Rings of the 'seam needle'. Obviously the 'central needle' is a much later addition of less consequence than the other two needles, and usually inserted between them.

On a very large lo p'an there may be a subdivision of the 360 degrees of the circle included on the 'central needle'. This, because of its Jesuit origins, is a sufficient indication of the modernity of the 'central needle'. However, because

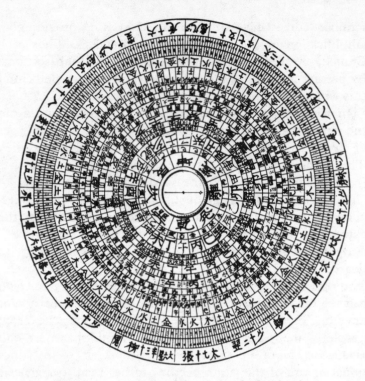

Figure 14 Analysis of the rings of a full lo p'an

of the sheer physical difficulty of subdividing the Ring into 360 sectors it is more usual for this Ring to be moved out beyond the Plate system to the penultimate Ring along with the unevenly divided hsiu (which rely upon it to help indicate how many degrees each hsiu occupies). These outer Rings are clearly defined in Figure 14, a compass examined by De Groot (1892, vol. 3:958). Note that the Ring numbering in Figure 14 commences at the centre with the Heaven Pool according to the Chinese convention, and is therefore one number out of step with De Groot's explanation of the Rings.

6

Making the compass work

The sun has gone through its degrees, the moon through its conjunctions, the stars returned to their stems, the year will soon begin again.

from *Li Chi* (Book of Rites)

The compass is used by the feng-shui practitioner to take bearings on the points where various landscape formations, dragons, or rivers appear to terminate, disappear, enter or leave the landscape, from the point of view where the reading is taken.

The needle is aligned either with the red hair-line drawn on the bottom of the needle housing, or by orientating the trigrams in Ring 2 of the compass to their correct quarters (for example Ch'ien trigram will be located in the south if using the Former Heaven Sequence).

Each limb of the dragon, knob, promontory, pool, water-course or man-made object has its bearings taken by a red thread with two weights on it which is draped over the compass, passing through the centre, and aligned with the object being sighted. The various segments of the compass which the thread crosses indicate the connection between the site under consideration and the feature whose bearing is being taken. Such 'bearings' are taken of every significant landform feature visible from the hsüeh. It is the interaction of these bearings which produces the 'luck' or otherwise of the site.

Thus the direction of the dragon veins, especially where they come to a head, which may be a cliff or the end of a line of hills, the position of pools or lines of drainage, levees, intersections of rivers (even paths, railway tracks and existing architectural lines) must be taken into account, as each may carry some part of the flow of ch'i through the landscape. On flat land, woods, boulders or large trees may mark the passage of ch'i through the earth, although these areas do not have the vigour of mountains or sloped sites which have more of the primal Yang energy of the ch'i. Wells and springs, as they indicate the eyes and ears of the dragon, are especially important features.

The three Plates of the compass indicate different facets of the site: the outer or Heaven Plate governs, among other things, the richness or poorness of the ch'i flow; the Earth Plate is to be used in divining 'the dragon's pulse' and locating the veins and arteries of earth ch'i. The ch'i indications on the Earth Plate measure the relative health or otherwise of ch'i in the earth surrounding the point which is being checked by the compass.

The middle Plate, or Man Plate, is to be used to discover the influences of Heaven and Earth on those living at this site.

Ch'i, being the life-blood of the living earth, and in-directly of the creatures crawling upon its body, fluctuates in much the same way as the pulses of the human body. Traditional Chinese medicine has always been much concerned with the measurements of various pulses at different points in the anatomy, drawing deductions about the state of health from the differences between each pulse rate. It is a natural extension, therefore, to expect that the health of the earth can be determined by checking the pulse or cyclical phase of the ch'i. As ch'i concentrates and disperses, or grows, prospers and decays, a feng-shui practitioner needs to know at any point in space or time the cyclical phase of the ch'i. The different phases of ch'i are outlined on the Man Plate, and examined in Chapter 2.

Where there is 'ceasing ch'i', the way is left open for incursions of sha. Traditionally, half the compass contains directions which are prone to the ingress of sha, although this does not mean that sha is necessarily generated at these points, merely that a weakness or predisposition is implied which could be counteracted by a positive landform located in the direction indicated, like a strongly Yang mountain.

Obviously, especially in a city or suburban feng-shui reading, the features which are going to impinge on the site are road alignments, trees and adjoining high buildings, particularly those parallel with the building under scrutiny. Factors such as the line taken by adjoining rooftops, or the compass reading for any break in the skyline which might provide a ch'i entry or exit point should be taken.

If the site has a garden, then the orientation of the most prominent trees and shrubs should be considered. Serried rows of trees either side of a straight drive should be modified so that they curve, especially if the drive leads directly from the gate to the front entrance. If the doorstep and front gate are almost synonymous then the installation of a feng-shui tablet to deflect sha might be considered. Any suspected unfavourable direction can be diagnosed by examining the mutual destruction order to the five elements (see Chapter 4).

Thus a feature which might be classified under the element Metal will cause 'wasting away and injury' if placed in a Wood direction because 'Metal destroys Wood'. Thus 'Metal destroying Wood' means wasting away and 'Earth destroying Water' might indicate illness. 'Water destroying Fire' means death in youth while 'Fire destroying Metal' predisposes to natural calamities. Other calamities such as loss of office or lack of offspring may also be indicated. These elemental directions can be read either from the compass or directly off the Lo-shu diagram.

When using the compass indoors for the determination of the feng-shui qualities of a room or building, the disc of the compass should be inserted in its square base. Then the square base is placed parallel to the door or wall in question. Two pieces of red thread are bound across the disc from the centre mark to each side of the square base, thus bisecting the disc into four quarters. Now as the wall is not necessarily exactly on a cardinal bearing, these two threads will parallel the orientation of the building, whilst the disc of the compass is rotated until the south-pointing needle coincides with the red marking in the 'Heaven Pool' or needle well under the glass.

In this fashion the square base becomes the Earth Plate, or a microcosmic orientation of the building under consideration, while the Heaven disc of the compass turns to coincide with the compass points (albeit possibly influenced by local variations in declination).

The practitioner then ascertains where the red threads cut the disc and reads off an interpretation from this. At the simplest level, he may examine where the thread cuts the outermost circle of 360 degrees which are marked alternatively with black crosses or red circles indicating ill or good fortune. (Some of these points are neutral as well.) This will give a generalized indication of the propitiousness of the site. He follows this by selecting one of the three groups, Earth Plate, inner Heaven Plate or outer Heaven Plate, depending upon his purposes, but in the case of buildings most likely concentrating on the former, and reads off the precise bearing of the building in terms of the twenty-four azimuthal directional points, sixty dragons and relevant trigram (indicating special benefits for one or other member of the family concerned).

A third method of using the compass, and one which is more complex, is to choose one particularly prominent landscape feature with a very distinct form and align it with that part of the compass which corresponds to its nature. With this method the south-pointing needle does not necessarily align with the trigram ch'ien. The quarter, trigram, Stem and Branch that it does align with immediately become of overriding importance in the assessment of this spot. The assumption is that if the most prominent landscape form is aligned with the most appropriate point on the compass, then the rest of the alignments must also be correct. Now as the south is the most crucial point in the whole science of feng-shui, the characters to which the compass now points on this new setting will indicate the overall nature of the spot and consequently its suitability as a hsüeh or dragon's lair. Then each of the other quarters must be taken into account in turn. If at S 60 degrees W, for example, the predominant feature is a hare-shaped hill then the mao point (hare) would be orientated towards it leaving the south-seeking needle pointing to the ch'ou point. This gives the site the qualities of the later point, that is, those of an ox. The site is therefore very propitious for anyone born in the year of the ox, e.g. 1949 or 1961.

All the Rings which refer specifically to 'dragons' are for riding the ch'i and indicate which influences enter the site and at which times of the year.

Now we reach the crux and heart of the whole operation with the compass.

When it is decided which of the surrounding features or veins of ch'i is the most categorically auspicious, a siting is taken of it, and its sexagenary character is determined. From that the six days ($\frac{1}{60}$) of the year appropriate to the character are determined. Now if the burial or building takes place within these six days thenceforth the site is for ever connected with this source of ch'i.

It is rather like a turnstile which revolves one complete turn per year with an entrance which is open for six days to each of the sixty directions at any time and the influence of the ch'i from that point. If the burial takes place at the appropriate time when the 'turnstile' faces a beneficent and plentiful source of ch'i, this source of ch'i will continue to serve the grave or building for the whole of the year, not just six days a year, to the partial exclusion of all the other sources of ch'i or sha, good, bad or indifferent.

It is as if the opening of the grave, or in the case of a house, the settling of the roof beams, opens a specific ch'i vein which remains attached to and feeds the site from then on. It is easy to see how important it is to 'pounce' on the right time of the year to get access to the best ch'i vein the site has to offer.

If further accuracy is required, Ring 25 of the compass of

Wu Wang Kang breaks down each sexagenary character into six sections, being the lines of its hexagram, enabling accuracy to be increased to a one-day period.

If one wishes to improve the existing feng-shui influences of a place then this technique can be used to 'open' a new vein of beneficial ch'i by altering the flow of ch'i during the six chosen days.

Besides the use of the compass to determine the correct day or six-day period, there is also a need to apply data from the horoscope of the owner of the building together with the recommendations of the *Tung Sing*, or Chinese almanac or that particular month and year. The birthdate of the owner should not, for example, be at variance with the date indicated by the sexagenary character allotted to the ch'i vein with which it is proposed to connect the site.

It is necessary for the sexagenary character of a man's birth year to coincide with those of the site, but it is not so dangerous if the sexagenary characters of the month, day or hour are not compatible with those of the site. Until the birth year at least coincides, building or alteration to an existing feng-shui configuration should be postponed.

The initial complexity of the compass can be broken down by analysing one or two factors at a time. Similarly the apparent variance between the rings is a product of the three-Plate system and the fact that the compass bears in 'fossilized form' on its face practically every system of time or space enumeration of any importance at any time in China. Consequently some of the older rings are at variance with the newer ones. A good example is the ring of 365 days not quite measuring the same thing as the ring of 360 degrees, a concept which was introduced quite late into China by the Jesuits.

The important factor to remember is that the basic rings are categories which are multiples of twelve with the introduction of the five-element/ten-Stem category, and, at the heart of the compass, the eight trigrams.

7
Household feng-shui

Do not despise the snake because he has no horns for one day he may become a dragon.

Traditional Chinese proverb

Feng-shui not only applies to the landscape and town planning but also to individuals. Sometimes, for example, the redecoration of a room has a greater effect on its occupants than would be expected, and sometimes re-orientating a bed, perhaps through 90 degrees, can completely change one's sleep patterns.

Similarly a feng-shui practitioner can advise on the location of a new wall in the garden, the position of a statue or the erection of a tablet to ward off the malicious influences of 'secret arrows'. A student not doing well in his studies might be advised to move his desk to another quarter or to face a different direction, and the positioning of a sick-bed might make a difference which will enable the patient to recover more rapidly. Nor is this just the stimulus of a new view, it is as basic as the orientation of a plant towards light or away from it, so even a patient may flourish or fade according to his or her bed orientation. With correct feng-shui orientation he or she can take advantage of positive, healing natural forces.

Feng-shui hsien-sheng are trained to use both their instinctive feelings for the changing patterns of the landscape as well as special compass equipment to diagnose the prevailing good or bad influences and their likely effects on any particular man-made or natural structure.

One of the classics of feng-shui is the *Yang Chai*, or 'Yang Dwelling Manual', dealing especially with the siting of houses (not graves, for Yang dwellings are the house of the living). The *Yang Chai* gives over a hundred diagrams with text and commentary showing many different situations and combinations of architectural features including trees, roads, temples, graves, paths and mounds. The general rules applying to different situations are explained at the beginning of the book, while the whole of the last section deals with houses sited inauspiciously in relation to temples and monasteries and with those houses whose inhabitants' children have little success in school, examinations or jobs.

The *Yang Chai* also recommends various 'talismans' with instructions for their preparation such as the kind of ink, size and type of board to be used to neutralize or overcome certain exceptional situations which could occur at particular times of the year. A typical talisman might be inscribed with 'T'ai-shan dares to resist (the evil influences)', thus invoking the might of China's most celebrated mountain chain to fend off sha (noxious vapours) and kuei (various kinds of demons). It is typically written in red by a Taoist priest on a peachwood board some fourteen inches in length. Its setting up might be accompanied by a sacrifice of food, drink or incense. These talismans are specified as an auxiliary aid to the usages of feng-shui and are more like a stop-gap than a permanent solution to a particular feng-shui siting problem.

Much of the talismanic usage is common to general Taoist Chinese practice and therefore not worth elaborating on here, but to understand many of the rules of household feng-shui it is necessary to have a rough idea of the design of a traditional Chinese house.

Like the body, any house has orifices, doors and windows which need to take in the flow of ch'i which must then circulate without stagnating to enable the house to 'breathe'. However, these openings must be well guarded against the direct ingress of any 'secret arrows' generated by adjoining buildings or street alignments.

Typical Chinese houses, especially those described by Hsü (1971) in Yunnan, are one- or two-storeyed structures arranged around a central courtyard. The more ambitious households have two adjoining courtyards. Most are made of brick and stone and white or yellow lime plaster with tiled roofs and floors made of wood or brick.

The main door of the family home usually faces south or east. More complicated versions sometimes have a series of three interconnecting doors which alternatively enter from the east, south and east as the guest comes through to the central courtyard, facing each direction in turn. The doors sometimes have elaborately hand-carved woodwork and are surmounted by decorative lintels, sometimes with a wooden structure or a sort of tiled cover with wing-like projections similar to the roof of a pagoda. Quite often a wall, un-breached by windows, surrounds the entire house so that only one main entrance is apparent, and this is often flanked or blocked by a 'shadow wall' which prevents the direct access in a straight line of any sha or evil influence.

As a rule there are three rooms on each side of the four sides enclosing the courtyard which is usually paved with stone slabs. Ground-floor rooms are the living quarters of the family and the central room on each side is usually a reception or living room, with the two flanking rooms often being used as bedrooms. At each corner with a small opening on to the courtyard are the kitchens or service rooms carefully tucked away so as not to be too obvious. A covered way at this level provides veranda space around the perimeter of the courtyard.

On the second floor level, the most important room is the ancestral shrine which traditionally takes the central room on the west side, while the rest of the rooms are usually store-rooms or subsidiary bedrooms. The ancestral shrine receives daily an offering of incense and one or two dishes of simple food, with more elaborate celebrations on the fifteenth day of the seventh moon, and various other festivals of the ancestors throughout the year.

The feng-shui aspects of the lower floor are carefully

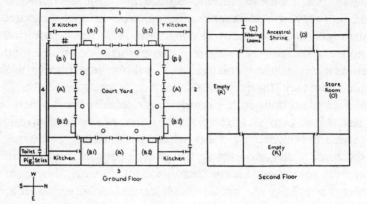

Figure 15 Typical Chinese house plans

considered in allocating the bedrooms for the various members of the extended family, the best going to the most
important member of the family. Best, however, does not
always mean the most attractive room for living in, but the
most auspicious, from the point of feng-shui orientation.
Conformity to traditional house design is to a large degree a
symptom of competition for family superiority, where the
residences were not so much considered as places to house
individual members in comfort and ease, but as signs of
unity and social prestige for the family group as a whole,
both the living and the dead.

A typical double courtyard household would have its
main entrance from the south side, with the ancestral shrine
and best bedrooms possibly in the west, with kitchen and
service facilities at the corners. The rooms dividing the two
courtyards are open in both directions to permit access
through them, and the subsidiary door might open to the
east. However there would seldom be a main entrance
leading to the north as this would permit the access of sha
or the cold winds of the north – a practical consideration as
well as one of feng-shui. Such entrances have sometimes
been bricked up on the advice of a feng-shui hsien-sheng.

Because of the idea of an extended family with room left for the developing lineage, Chinese houses are often too large for the families currently occupying them. It is usual practice to build a basic courtyard and then fill in the rooms along each side starting in the north and the west, so that the house is well 'backed', later adding a second court-yard or a second floor. Often the house's extension out-strips the growth of a prosperous family.

Quite often the rooms on the ground floor which are the most used are too dark because of the broad covered cor-ridors extending in front of them. The internal courtyard itself with rooms on all four sides gives little opportunity for the sun to enter the room because it is screened by the projecting veranda roofing. The covered corridors which extend around the house quite often on the southern side also help to promote bad ventilation, although probably originally they were an insulation and security measure.

Following the same theme, guests were often unable to enter the house directly, but had a skirt round the shadow wall designed to repel the direct approach of sha or demons. The shadow wall is a separate segment of wall about as high as the others but standing alone and opposite the main portal to the family home. Sometimes the family has two or three such walls each standing opposite to one of the several portals, and on each of these is quite often inscribed four large characters 'confirming' the good feng-shui of the household, and screening it from any damaging outside influences. Thus an act of sympathetic magic is linked with a practical protection.

Maybe the architectural background to the shadow wall owes its origin to military strategic design, when the wall would have served to prevent a large number of armed men entering the household at any one time. Perhaps the prac-tical exigency was generalized to the point where the protec-tion became symbolically important as well.

Obviously poor homes have few of these complicated architectural features, and depend largely upon written characters and hanging plaques to defend their doorways, which in the poorest case lead directly into the family shrine without benefit of a deflecting screen or wall.

How do these building conventions apply to Western-style houses? Assuming, for example, that the site is in the country rather than in a city, where major changes are probably precluded, there are a number of alterations that can be made in accordance with the precepts of feng-shui.

First, if possible the main orientation should be southwards (in the northern hemisphere) so that the general orientation of garden or main entrance could be adjusted accordingly. If there is no range of hills to the north of the site then the planting of a row of trees on this side can be beneficial. These will help absorb any sha generated by the site as well as protecting the site from the Yin influences of the north.

In southern China every house, hamlet and village lacking the necessary hill configuration has a small grove of bamboos or trees behind it for this purpose and a pond in front (to the south). If possible a pond with running water and a rather tortuous drainage system could be created in the same fashion especially if the site is lucky enough to slope down towards the south. Sometimes a pagoda replaces the pond – not quite as practical!

If your garden is laid out in a square fashion maybe the introduction of a little imagination to give it more natural lines could work wonders. Specifically, a straight path to the front door is highly undesirable: try re-laying it with curves.

More technical operations could include placing an octagonal board with the trigrams and Yang-Yin symbols painted on it opposite your front gate, or the positioning of stone lions or pottery dragons at strategic positions could further modify the accumulation of ch'i, but as Eitel says, 'by far the best and most effective means is to engage a geomancer, to do what he says, and to pay him well' – a counsel of perfection in the West!

Many modern Chinese texts on feng-shui are concerned with urban feng-shui: the location of houses and the orientation of their rooms. A number of popular texts written along these lines are currently circulating in Hong Kong and Taiwan. A selection of rules to be observed in the construction or purchase of a house (almost a house buyer's guide to feng-shui) could be excerpted from such manuals. Figure 16 is taken from a book published in Hong Kong and Singapore called 'A Simplified Guide to the Secrets of Feng-shui', the *Chan Wing Tai*. This and two books by Chan Ming Chai called *Can Feng-shui be believed?* (Hong Kong, 1977) and *How to Check the Feng-shui* (also published in Hong Kong) are representative of a number of such similar manuals which are often illustrated in a very simplified graphical form which verges on the cartoon.

The first category of rules concerns the circumstances or environment of the house; among these, for example, it is suggested that the mouth of a valley where it forms a fan-shaped delta is a most dangerous feng-shui situation. Likewise downstream from such a location is also inauspicious. To build or buy a house which has a large tree directly in front of the doorway is not only inconvenient but considered to be overpoweringly bad feng-shui, as it deflects the 'entry of wealth'. It is also considered inauspicious to build or buy a house situated on a triangular piece of land. If the house is lucky enough to have a central courtyard, then one should be careful not to have a tree or pond located at the exact centre of the courtyard because it detracts from the ch'i accumulation of the house itself.

The arrangement of the rooms and facilities within the house (Figure 16), as we have seen, is not only traditional but hedged around with a number of taboos. The most obvious stipulation is that the primary rooms that are used most often should, like the house, face south (Figure 16a). Failing this, the master bedroom should be located in the centre of the house (on the southern side.).

If a premises is to be used as a shop, it should be certain not to face either the north-east or south-west. If a residential property, the kitchen should for preference face east, and certainly not south-west which is the most inauspicious location for a kitchen.

A

。處心中宅住於置配宜，間房的人主

B

。面東南在設宜房人老

C

在樹林地宜築建住房，地下
不要留有樹的殘根。

Figure 16 Household feng-shui

The eldest members of the family should, if possible, have rooms facing on the south-east, not in the primary direction of the south which should be allocated to the head of the family, but as they are potential ancestors they should have at least the next compromise position of a south-east orientation (Figure 16b).

Obviously practical suggestions, such as that a house without a rear door is dangerous, although subsumed under the heading of feng-shui, seem to be more in the province of common sense. Other regulations would delight the heart of a council health inspector in any country, for it is suggested that a bedroom should not open directly on to a kitchen, nor that a toilet should face directly on the main entrance of the house.

A particularly Chinese restriction is that the family altar should not be observable from the street – not only does it lower respect for the family, but it also leaves the family tutelary god open to attack or ridicule from the public.

Constructional rules which are a combination of common structural good sense and feng-shui rationale include stipulations that one should not build on top of a buried well. This is not only because wells were regarded as sacred places, but because, from a feng-shui point of view, to fill up wells in order to build one's house is the equivalent of closing the breathing orifices of the dragon and will encourage sickness of the eyes or ears of those living in the house.

Similarly it is advised that one should not construct, renovate or reconstruct a house in which one of the members is pregnant, as the forces of the cosmos are considered to be adequate only for the bringing to birth of one child, or house, at a time.

If you survey the site before building, then be sure that there is no decayed tree stump lurking under the soil, for this is an extremely inauspicious feng-shui indication which will blight any house built above it. The theory is that the thwarted growth of the tree will take out its frustration on the newly 'grown' house by blighting its occupants (Figure 16c).

In terms of construction materials, it is considered to be not only aesthetically unpleasant but also inauspicious to use timber as vertical beams in the reverse direction to which they grew during their life as trees. If the grain of the wood and the natural direction of growth point upwards, then those in the household will increase in prosperity rather than the opposite.

There is much talk about the relationship between facilities in a house in such manuals, and most of the suggestions are counsels of perfection in terms of the allocation of living space, but have their roots in common sense. It is, for example, bad feng-shui to connect either two bedrooms (the loss of independence of the occupants) or two bathrooms. Bedrooms should never be built over either empty spaces, garages or empty store-rooms as this creates a ch'i vacuum underneath and affects the occupant adversely.

The gateway of the house should, by the same rule, not be bigger than the entrance way to the house, for it thereby detracts from the ch'i accumulation of the household, but there should be ample room in front of any garage entrance.

Of course the general rules which equate water with Yin and fire with Yang, and which suggest that they do not confront each other, not only help the householder in his choice of functions for individual rooms, but are also a general rule of feng-shui. You will remember that Yang should in each case predominate over Yin to obtain a favourable feng-shui balance.

The home-orientated rules can also be applied to public buildings. Not only is a person's destiny and well-being affected by where he lives or where he buries his ancestors, but it is also affected by where he works and where he worships. Consequently the correct feng-shui location of temples was of the utmost importance. In Hong Kong alone, for example, there are in excess of 600 temples, mostly Buddhist or Taoist, serving a population of 4.4 million.

Obviously in such an overcrowded area the demands of modern life and building regulations have led to many temples being built in areas not considered completely auspicious from a feng-shui point of view. To counteract this, mirrors are often put into windows or doorways to reflect 'secret arrows'. Because of the maritime nature of Hong Kong, a number of temples are not located on the pulse of the dragon but 'in front of a dragon stretching down from hill to sea'. This means that these temples are situated between two spurs of a hill on a slope down to a valley or directly opening onto the sea. A particularly good example is the Tin Hau's temple at Joss House Bay.

The traditional Chinese temple consists of three main halls, each leading into the other. At the front entrance is the bell tower where the temple's bell and drum should be kept. Behind this is the smoke tower, where paper offerings are burned in huge urns, the smoke from which rises and escapes – theoretically – through an opening in the roof of this tower formed by pillars elevating its roof above the other roofing. Directly behind this is the main palace, with its altars and images of the temple's principal gods. Many temples have side halls to accommodate the minor deities, usually attached to which are quarters for the temple-keeper and his family.

The main altars themselves are effectively at the back, or north side, of the temple with the entrance opening on to the auspicious south. The most modern temples seem to have dispensed with the bell tower and smoke tower, preferring a more practical external incinerator partly to eliminate fire risk and partly to reduce the smoke-blackening of the ceilings.

The roofs of the temples are their most ornate feature, as these are responsible for the interaction of the temple with the elements and the wind. The ridges are richly decorated and encrusted with figures representing divinities and folk heroes often made of porcelain. The colouring is also symbolic: red for happiness; green for peace and eternity; white also for peace and occasionally for mourning; with gold for royalty, strength and wealth. The predominance of gold and red in Chinese culture speaks for itself.

The central symbol of the temple's rooms and much of the interior decoration is of course the dragon which pursues the flaming dragon pearl. The rippling carvings of dragons on the lines of the roof are designed to stimulate the flow of the dragon force, the ch'i, into the temple itself. Subsidiary temple animal symbolism includes the carp (with its ability to swim upstream against the flow of water) and the owl's tail.

The second most important Chinese symbolic animal, the lion, portrayed in a highly stylized form (for it is some time since lions were known in China) acts as temple door guardian and guardian of the altars. Lions were in fact introduced into China by Buddhists from India, and during their relatively brief appearance engendered many myths.

In the home, carvings of the sacred animals are used for much the same purposes, with lions particularly being used as portal guardians. The same stress that is laid upon colour in the temple also applies to the home where ill-aspected rooms should be decorated with strong colours like red or gold on the carpets or tapestry, and perhaps the occasional black-painted door.

Red is used as it is symbolic of happiness and prosperity, gold for its obvious symbolism, yellow for gaiety, and green for a quiet atmosphere. However, you should be careful that no red wall faces west nor black one faces south, as black is the colour of the north which must not be made to confront its opposite. Any particularly oppressive or small rooms should be painted in light shades.

The moving of furniture to positions which do not obstruct the circular flow of ch'i from room to room is also an important consideration. The object is to bring the environment into tune with the psyche of its occupants and to make the best of influences impinging on the house from outside. In a rural setting modification or collaboration with nature predominates, while in the city the desire to deflect the many conflicting influences predominates.

Finally, each window and door should be considered from the point of view of the inflowing ch'i which should be led by the general lines of the furnishings in a spiral from room to room before it exhausts itself. No room should be cut off from the rest of the house in such a way that it can become a repository for stagnant ch'i. The converse of this is true: that a room with too many doors is not only draughty in the physical sense but is liable to be a disperser of ch'i. Consideration should be given to sealing up one or two of the doors to such a room. It should also be easy to move from room to room without bumping into the corners of protruding furnishings, for the flow of the ch'i is very much like the movements of a dancer who will not perform well on a cluttered stage. Such judgements, although to an extent subjective, can be checked against the compass sightings from the middle of each room, through its window(s) to the most prominent or powerful visible feature. If the reading (for that year) is a good one, then that room should be paid more attention. If on the other hand the sighting is not good then the room could be supplied with a 'deflector'. If the sighting is fairly neutral, then the emphasis is upon guiding the ch'i through the room.

Obviously, with the rotation of the Stems and the Branches, each year will bring new influences, and hence new thoughts, to bear upon each room. Even with the changing seasons your appreciation of the changing feng-shui environment in terms of both time and space will be expanded.

A short feng-shui vocabulary

an chien	'secret arrow'; a bad influence in the form of a line aimed at a site, such as a path seen at a distance, or the line of a roof, if directed towards a site.
chen wu	structure intended to ward off evil influences, such as a pagoda or stone lion.
ch'i	life-breath, which is accumulated or dispersed by the form of the earth.
ching	classic.
fa	the feng-shui pattern of the landscape.
feng	wind.
feng sha	noxious wind.
feng-shui hsien-sheng	a practitioner of feng-shui.
ho-t'u	a magic square connected with the Former Heaven Sequence of trigrams. See also Lo-shu.
hsing	elements, but literally 'to move'.
hsüeh	lair of the dragon – site with an accumulation of ch'i.
hsiu	constellations.
hsün lung	to seek the dragon, by feng-shui rules, which belongs to and surrounds a grave site.
hua	change.
hun	part of the soul which joins its ancestors.
I Ching	Book of Changes.

kan-yü	old name for feng-shui.
kan-yü chia	a practitioner of kan-yü.
kua	the trigrams of the *I Ching*.
kuei	demons.
lo ching	the feng-shui compass having a magnetic needle, the cardinal points, and various circles divided into eighths, twelfths, and multiples of these.
lo p'an	feng-shui compass.
Lo-shu	a magic square of numbers connected with the Later Heaven Sequence of trigrams.
luo pan	feng-shui compass.
lung	dragon.
lung mei	dragon veins.
lung shen	dragon spirits.
mao	due east.
ming t'ang	bright hall, the pool in front and to the south of the site.
pa kua	eight trigrams of the *I Ching*.
p'o	part of the soul which remains in the grave.
sha	earth or alluvial formations, noxious breath, literally 'sand'.
sha ch'i	noxious ch'i.
shan	mountains.
shan-shui	landscape in both painting and feng-shui sense, literally 'mountain waters'.
shen	spirits.
shih erh chih	the twelve cyclic characters or twelve Earthly Branches. Also called ti chih.
shin erh kung	the Twelve Palaces, or phases of ch'i.
shih kan	the ten cyclic characters called the Heavenly Stems or Pillars of Heaven. Also called t'ien kan.
shui	water and watercourses.
shui-lung	water dragon.

t'ai-shi	Great Absolute.
t'ai yang	the sun.
t'ai yin	the moon.
tang	a flat low space before a tomb.
ti	earth.
t'ien	heaven.
ti li	doctrine of earth. Geography. Often used for feng-shui.
trigram	one of the eight constituent figures found in the *I Ching* made up of three Yin or Yang lines.
ts'eng	rings of the compass.
t'u	earth.
tuan kang	practitioner or priest of wu chiao, a magician.
tzu	due north.
wu	due south.
wu hsing	the five elements.
Yang	male.
yang chai	Yang dwelling (house).
Yin	female.
yin chai	Yin dwelling (tomb).
yu	due west.

Select bibliography

BENNETT, STEVEN J. (1978), 'Patterns of the sky and earth: the Chinese science of applied cosmology', in *Chinese Science*, vol. 3, pp. 1–26, University of Pennsylvania.

CHU, W. K. and SHERRILL, W. A. (1976), *The Astrology of I Ching*, Routledge & Kegan Paul, London.

DE GROOT, J. J. M. (1897), *The Religious System of China*, vol. 3, bk I, pt III, ch. XII, pp. 935–1056, Brill, Leiden.

DORÉ, H. (SJ) (1914–33), *Researches into Chinese Superstition* (trans. M. Kennelly), vol. IV, pp. 402–16, T'usewei Printing Press, Shanghai, 10 vols.

EDKINS, J. (1872), 'Feng-shui', in *Chinese Recorder and Missionary Journal*, Foochow, March.

EITEL, E. J. (1873), *Feng-shui: or the Rudiments of Natural Science in China*, Trubner, London, reprinted Cokaygne, Cambridge, 1973.

FEUCHTWANG, STEPHAN D. R. (1974), *An Anthropological Analysis of Chinese Geomancy*, Vithagna, Laos.

FREEDMAN, MAURICE (1966), *Chinese Lineage and Society: Fukien and Kwangtung*, Athlone, London.

FREEDMAN, MAURICE (1969), 'Geomancy', in *Proceedings of the Royal Anthropological Institute of Great Britain and Ireland* (1968 Presidential Address), pp. 5–18, Athlone, London.

HAYES, J. (1967), 'Geomancy and the Village', in *Some Traditional Chinese Ideas and Conceptions in Hong Kong Social Life Today*, Hong Kong: Royal Asiatic Society (Hong Kong Branch), Hong Kong.

HSÜ, FRANCIS L. K. (1971), *Under the Ancestors' Shadow* (revised), Stanford University Press.

KAN, C. Y. (1968–9), 'Feng-Shui, its Implications on Chinese Architecture', thesis, Hong Kong University.

LEBRA, W. P. (1966), *Okinawan Religion: Belief, Ritual and Social Structure*, University of Hawaii Press, Honolulu.

LEGEZA, LASZLO (1975), *Tao Magic: the Secret Language of Diagrams and Calligraphy*, Thames & Hudson, London.

LEGGE, JAMES (trans.) (1979), *Yi-King: The Book of Changes*, Clarendon Press, Oxford.

LIP MONG HAR, EVELYN (1979), *Chinese Geomancy*, Times Books International, Singapore.

MARCH, ANDREW L. (1968), 'An Appreciation of Chinese Geomancy', in *Journal of Asian Studies*, XXVII, pp. 253–67, February.

MARTEL, FRANÇOIS (1971), 'Analyse formelle de configurations symboliques chinoises', Diplôme de l'École Pratique des Hautes Etudes, Paris.

MARTEL, FRANÇOIS (1972), 'Les boussoles divinatoires chinoises, in *Communications*, vol. 19, Paris.

MAYER, JEFFREY F. (1976), *Peking as a Sacred City*, Chinese Association for Folklore, Taipei.

NEEDHAM, JOSEPH (1956, 1959, 1962), *Science and Civilisation in China*: vol. 2, *History of Scientific Thought*; vol. 3, *Mathematics and the Sciences of the Heavens and the Earth*; vol. 4, pt 1, *Physics*, Cambridge University Press.

RAWSON, P. and LEGEZA, L. (1973), *Tao*, Thames & Hudson, London.

SHERRILL, W. A. and CHU, W. K. (1977), *An Anthology of I Ching*, Routledge & Kegan Paul, London.

SKINNER, STEPHEN (1977), *The Oracle of Geomancy: Divination by Earth*, Warner Destiny, New York.

SKINNER, STEPHEN (1980), *Terrestrial Astrology: Divination by Geomancy*, Routledge & Kegan Paul, London.

WHEATLEY, PAUL (1971), *The Pivot of the Four Quarters*, Aldine, Chicago.

Since the first publication of the present book, interest in feng-shui *has increased and the following have been published:*

DE KERMADEC, JEAN-MICHEL (1983), *The Way to Chinese Astrology*, Unwin, London.

PALMER, MARTIN (editor) (1986), *T'ung Shu: the Ancient Chinese Almanac*, Rider, London.

ROSSBACH, SARAH (1983), *Feng Shui*, Hutchinson, London.

ROSSBACH, SARAH (1987), *Interior Design with Feng Shui*, Century, London.

WALTERS, DEREK (1987), *Chinese Astrology*, Aquarian Press, Wellingborough.

WALTERS, DEREK (1988), *Feng Shui*, Pagoda, London.

Index

ARKANA – NEW-AGE BOOKS FOR MIND, BODY AND SPIRIT

With over 150 titles currently in print, Arkana is the leading name in quality new-age books for mind, body and spirit. Arkana encompasses the spirituality of both East and West, ancient and new, in fiction and non-fiction. A vast range of interests are covered, including Psychology and Transformation, Health, Science and Mysticism, Women's Spirituality and Astrology.

If you would like a catalogue of Arkana books, please write to:

Arkana Marketing Department
Penguin Books Ltd
27 Wright's Lane
London W8 5TZ